ARATOR'S On the Acts of the Apostles
(De Actibus Apostolorum)

Richard J. Schrader,
Editor and Translator

Joseph L. Roberts III and John F. Makowski,
Co-Translators

Scholars Press
Atlanta, Georgia

THE AMERICAN ACADEMY OF RELIGION
CLASSICS IN RELIGIOUS STUDIES

ARATOR'S On the Acts of the Apostles

Library of Congress Cataloging-in-Publication Data

Arator, Subdiaconus, fl. 513-544.
Arator's De actibus apostolorum.

(Classics in religious studies ; no. 6)
Translation from the Latin.
Includes bibliographies.
1. Bible. N.T. Acts—History of Biblical events—Poetry. 2. Christian poetry, Latin—Translations into English. 3. Epic poetry, Latin—Translations into English. 4. Christian poetry, English—Translations from Latin. 5. Epic poetry, English—Translations from Latin. I. Schrader, Richard J. II. Title. III. Title: De actibus apostolorum. IV. Series.
PA 6220.A19D413 1987 873'.01 87-9661

ISBN 1-555-40133-3 (alk. paper)

ARATOR'S On the Acts of the Apostles

THE AMERICAN ACADEMY OF RELIGION
CLASSICS IN RELIGIOUS STUDIES

Carl A. Raschke, Editor

Classics in Religious Studies, No. 6
ARATOR'S On the Acts of the Apostles

Richard J. Schrader, Editor and Translator
Joseph L. Roberts III and John F. Makowski, Co-Translators

CONTENTS

Introduction

Arator and His Epic

Arator's *De Actibus Apostolorum*[1] is not the most representative of the early Christian epics, and certainly it is not the finest, having been called, among other things, "the worst of poems on an excellent subject," one that marks a "decline of culture."[2] These judgments, however, are too harsh, and they were not shared by the Venerable Bede, who has a place in the McKinlay edition's impressive list of medieval *testimonia*. Bede used Arator frequently, acknowledging in the preface of *Actuum Apostolorum Expositio* that

> me . . . maxime juvavit . . . qui ipsum ex ordine librum heroico carmine percurrens nonnullos in eodem metro allegoriae flores admiscuit . . . .
> [he has aided me most, who going through the same book chapter by chapter in heroic poetry, added not a few flowers of allegory in the same meter.][3]

Such features made the work popular in medieval curricula and have caused its decline in our own. Regrettably, the poem is not studied often, either for its own sake or for its influence on subsequent literature. The transformations of Virgil in the Christian-Latin epics were highly valued, but not a great deal has been done to associate them with early vernacular poetry, much of which is heroic, despite the widespread knowledge of these epics in the centers of learning that educated native poets.[4] The change in attitudes has depreciated the hybrid genre Arator chose, even though it had a long, distinguished history. Moreover, none of the Latin fathers wrote a commentary on Acts, and so *De Actibus* is uniquely valuable as the only extended treatment of its subject in the West prior to Bede.

Most of the dates in Arator's life, including those of his birth and death, are uncertain, but it is known that he was of Ligurian parentage and was trained in Milan, Pavia, and Ravenna.[5] A noted orator, he came to the attention of Theodoric and was given high office by his successor, Athalaric. Later, as a subdeacon in Rome, he composed the two books of his epic in the middle of the terrible war between Justinian and the Gothic rulers of Italy (536-54). This war featured three sieges of Rome, and it was apparently during one of these (537) that Arator took orders. He dedicated *De Actibus* to Pope Vigilius and gave a public reading, one of the last of its kind (April and May 544), in the appropriate setting of S. Petrus ad Vincula. The work was well received; thanks to encores it took four days to read.

The poem, without precedent in its choice of subject for epic treatment, demanded of its hearers a good knowledge of Acts and of the Bible generally. But while the principal events in Luke's account are covered, the only prominent apostles are Peter and Paul. Moreover, the literal level is everywhere the vehicle (or excuse) for searching out spiritual meanings. In this he outdid Sedulius, whom he imitated and frequently echoed. The three verse *epistolae* surrounding the work give an idea of Arator's aims.[6] For instance, the dedication to Pope Vigilius explains that mystical meanings will be drawn from the historical level, and, following the teaching of Jerome that parts of the Bible were written in verse,[7] it claims authority for the poem by way of the Hebrew tradition. The whole is concluded by a letter to the noble Parthenius, *Magister Officiorum*, which contains autobiographical information (such as his having been made a sheep when he was tonsured [69-70]) and remarks on his craft. Looking back, he tells how Parthenius used to recite poets

> In quibus ars fallax, pompa superba fuit (42)
> [in whom was a deceitful art, a proud display],

but that worthy also turned to the likes of Ambrose and Sidonius,

> veros . . . vates
> Quorum metra fides ad sua iura trahit. (43-44)
> [true bards whose lute draws the meters to its own laws.]

(By this rhetorical device Pope Gregory the Great snubbed the rules of Donatus and Bede explained the licenses of Sedulius.)[8] Following convention, Arator says that he wrote frivolous verse in his youth and that his friend counselled him thus:

> "O utinam malles" dixisti "rectius huius
> Ad Domini laudes flectere vocis iter!
> Ut quia nomen habes quo te vocitamus, Arator,
> Non abstrusa tibi sit sed aperta seges." (55-58)
> ["Oh, would that you had chosen more properly to turn the path of this voice toward praises of the Lord! so that, as you have the name by which we call you, Arator ('farmer'), the crop might not have been hidden, but instead accessible to you."]

Aside from his wide reading in the Christian classics, Arator was extremely well acquainted with the language and conventions of his pagan predecessors. He echoes or borrows from them constantly. But he has abandoned much that would place him in their company, *De Actibus* being something of an extreme in its genre. *Fatum* and *fortuna* do not appear, and all uses of *sors* are more or less neutral. The word *pietas* is without classical suggestions. From the opening—twenty lines on Christ's descent to hell and resurrection, which do not appear in Acts—a different tone is struck. Witke has remarked upon the abstractness of the passage, how it shows Arator's characteristic fascination with concepts. The mystical sense carries the narration, not vice versa.

> In short, Arator has moved from epic of the Latin tradition to a cosmological poetry which has little except form to do with the ancient genre. His rarified and most high-styled language has lost touch with earthly things in order better to narrate spiritual truths. One may see this beginning already in Sedulius, but Arator takes farther this tendency to deposit the significance in the implication rather than in the fact, and to sidestep factual narration altogether. The stories are agreed-upon conventions; the poet need only sketchily situate the event, and then can launch a full-scale interpretative evocation of it.[9]

Some formal elements of epic story-telling remain, as we shall see, but the characters and events in the narrative are swamped by abstractions.

The poem is of course hexametrical, and "pagan" diction is scattered throughout.[10] Heaven is Olympus, its ruler the *regnator/rector Olympi* out of Virgil and Lucan: Paul puts the phrase in the mouth of an angel at one point (2.1117). God is also called the familiar *Tonans*, as when Peter's prayer for Tabitha is said to reach the Thunderer (1.824). Hell is Avernus or Tartara, the *Tartara maesta* conquered by Christ and featured in an underworld vision in Lucan (1.183; *Pharsalia* 6.782).

Without *fama volat per urbem* (cf. 2.662-63 and *Ad Parthenium* 27) it would almost not be an epic of any sort. A good many quotations and echoes of the classics were doubtless unconscious, but judging such cases is difficult. Too many have intriguing parallels in the context of the original and were probably designed to provide a pleasurable shock of recognition. Arator defends women against the charge that something in their nature makes them *all* like Eve, explaining how the second Eve (Mary) made up for the first by bringing us Christ (1.59-68). His language in justifying the happy fall (62-63) is nearly identical to that of the ironical Lucan when he said that even crimes like the civil war were not too high a price—for gaining Nero! (*Phars*. 1.37-38). Arator remarks, as a successor to Judas is about to be chosen,

> Nunc opus est votis. (1.103)
> [Now there is need for prayers.]

To this the closest echo is the characteristic (and opposite) statement of Caesar as he tells his men to take fate in their own hands: "Nil opus est votis" (*Phars.* 7.252). Peter advises the Jews to flee their sins ("Sed fugite, o miseri") in words used long before to warn against the Cyclops (1.188; *Aeneid* 3.639). Gold provides gifts (1.416), but then so did the Greeks (*Aen.* 2.49). Embellishing Paul's imprisonment (Acts 16), Arator says,

> Tota concurritur urbe
> Qui primus nova tecta petat quive oscula figat
> Postibus et tacta sacretur parte cylindri. (2.411-13)
> [There is a rush in the whole city to be the first to seek the remade building, or to plant a kiss on the door-posts and be blessed by touching part of the bolt.]

His language manages to recall three episodes from the classics, while also reversing the unfavorable connotations of the original situations: the actions of hysterical women in Priam's palace (*Aen.* 2.489-90), at Latium (7.393), and at Lemnos (Valerius Flaccus, *Argonautica* 2.168-69). When seven Jews try to expel a demon, they

> nova proelia temptant (2.642)
> [attempt strange battles],

as had Aeneas' men against the Harpies (*Aen.* 3.240). And when Lucan says of a mutilated warrior that his valor (*virtus*) increased in adversity (*Phars.* 3.614), he means it either as a Stoic compliment or in reference to Homeric heroism. For Arator, however, the phrase *virtus / Crescit in adversis* (2.1103-04) applies to the Christian soldier, and he qualifies *virtus* with *mansura* (enduring).

The vocabulary associated with heroes, soldiers, and athletes is likewise transferred to the *miles Christi* and to Christ Himself. It is Christ the Victor who ascends to heaven.

> Nova pompa triumphi!
> Arva Deus petiit, homo sidera. (1.34-35)
> [A new procession of triumph! God has sought earth, man the stars.]

Thunder and the heavenly choir greet the approach of this *rector Olympi.* Attended by the "trophy" of His flesh, He places in heaven the "spoils" snatched out of hell (cf. 1.318-20). Diction of this nature is abundant, and it is put to its best use in the account of Stephen's martyrdom (1.586-623). He was the first to win the "palm" in this kind of contest (*agon*), his very name signifying his crown.[11] An exultant soldier (*miles ovans*), he is taken by Christ to his rewards as victor,

> Et per tot lapides petrae coniungitur uni.
> Quis furor iste novus, nulli feritate secundus,

> Parcere nolle pio! (1.600-02)
> [and through so many stones is joined to the One Rock. What strange fury is this (quoting Ascanius' words to the Trojan women who have burned the ships: *Aen.* 5.670), second to no one in ferocity, not to wish to spare a good man!]

But Christ,

> caro iuncta Tonanti (1.613)
> [the flesh joined to the Thunderer],

had been with him, for

> dux praescius armat
> Quos ad dona vocat. (1.614-15)
> [the General in His foreknowledge arms those whom He summons to gifts.][12]

Other favorite motifs of Christian poets are employed, and of these I will mention here just one, mankind's true *patria*. Arator's finest treatment of the subject involves a characteristic series of associations (2.551-68). Paul's craft was tentmaking; tents are handy for protecting wayfarers;

> Nos quoque per culpam prima de sede repulsi
> Exsilio mundi iacimur; via reddita tandem
> Qua patriae repetamus iter. (2.556-58)
> [We also, driven from our first home through sin, are scattered by exile in the world; the way by which we may begin again our journey to the fatherland has finally been given back.]

Therefore, we need the protection of Paul, whose earthly habitations are but shadows of the heavenly ones he raises.

This is the sort of thing which led Raby to assert that the poem "can hardly fail to weary a modern reader; but the Middle Ages loved it precisely for its mysticism and allegory, as they loved the *Psychomachia* of Prudentius and the *Carmen Paschale* of Sedulius."[13] Indeed, because of the quotable sententiae and the "mysticism" which it has been the modern affectation to despise, it is easy to see why Bede and others prized Arator so highly. A modern would have to confess that the frequent number symbolism is seldom engaging, and that it is not surprising to hear Christ in hell called the Ferryman of life (1.184) or to see Aquila (Acts 18:2) allegorized along the lines of the bestiary eagle (*aquila*) (2.528 ff.). But more often than not, Arator's metaphysical wit delights as much as it instructs, as in Peter's description of Judas' suicide by hanging:

> taedia noxae
> Horruit ipse suae stringens in gutture vocem
> Exemplo cessante ream, qui parte necari
> Promeruit qua culpa fuit, crimenque retractans

> Iudicio tali permisit membra furori
> Aeris ut medio communi poneret hosti
> Debita poena locum; caelo terraeque perosus
> Inter utrumque perit. (1.84-91)
> [he himself trembled at the loathsomeness of his offense, binding his unexampled, guilty voice in his throat; he deserved to be killed in that part where his fault was, and, retracting his crime by such a judgment, he gave his limbs up to such madness (suicide) that the penalty due to the common enemy fixed his position in the midst of the air; hated by heaven and earth, he perished between the two.]

Bede would also have appreciated his treatment of paganism, which is generally harsh. Conversion and renewal are important themes in Arator, and perhaps this is why the section on the cure of the cripple at Lystra (Acts 14:7-19) is one of the longest in the poem. For when Paul works the miracle, he and Barnabas are called Mercury and Jupiter by the crowd. (Barnabas is omitted from the epic, as are the names of the gods.) Paul's restrained answer is lengthened in the poetic version (2.177-97) and perforce includes the moderate statement that God let former nations follow their ways. Arator further allows that Paul, the Apostle to the Gentiles, had as his mission the healing of people from whom God's word had been concealed (2.213-14). But he takes care to highlight passages in which idolatry is condemned (2.276-79; Acts 15:20) and to make some pagans more culpable than they are in the Bible. Where Scripture has Roman citizens protest Paul's teaching because to follow it would be against the law, Arator adds to their statement the claim that as strange rites enter the world the old gods are falling (2.399-402; Acts 16:20- 21).[14] During the apostle's famous encounter with the Athenians on the Areopagus, Paul is far more hostile in the poetic account than in the Biblical.[15]

The overall structure of *De Actibus* is simple. Like its original it has two major divisions. Book 1, dominated by Peter, generally follows the order of events in Acts 1-12; Book 2 covers the remaining sixteen chapters and is almost entirely given over to Paul. But while the two apostles are very prominent and are brought together at the end in such a way as to demonstrate unity of theme, it is not quite right to call them the poem's heroes. They are too often dissolved into the spiritual level, too often left behind so that Arator might be free to exercise his ingenuity and discover shadowings-forth of baptism. The true center of the poem is the descent of the Holy Spirit (1.119 ff.), and the true hero is God, as He is likewise the hero in all of "salvation history" and in the life of the individual Christian soldier. He is celebrated very often in the form of the Christ who conquered hell, but also, with much greater frequency, in the Third Person, the "fostering Spirit" (*almus Spiritus*) who granted the gift of tongues and is the source of inspiration for the Christian poet (cf. 1.225-29). The irrelevant Muses are utterly banished. Only the Spirit can make the poem worthy, not of the poet, but of Him (2.577-83).[16]

In the tradition of the rhetorical epic, the work is filled with meditative and gnomic passages.[17] A typical example of Arator's "digressive" technique is the story of Ananias (1.417-54; Acts 5:1-11). "Unlucky" (*infelix*) Ananias was destroyed because he attempted to deceive the apostles in regard to his profits. His wife suffered the same fate, the usual result of complicity in crime.

> Denique quando
> Auri cessat amor? qui pectora semper adurit,
> Quo capitur mortale genus, qua pullulat omne
> De radice malum, cuius violentius ardet
> Ambitio crescente modo, stimulantque rapinis
> Addita lucra famem. (1.422-27)
>
> [When finally will the love for gold cease? It always inflames hearts; the human race is captured by it; from this root every evil springs forth; ambition for it (gold) burns the more violently the more it grows; and added profits got by plunder stimulate hunger (for more).][18]

Peter accused Ananias of lying to God, the *Spiritus almus*. That other enemy of the Trinity, "unlucky" Arius, died with his bowels pouring forth.[19] So had Judas: both committed sacrilege with their mouths, the one by betraying the Trinity, the other by dividing it.

The organization of most sections is reminiscent of the associative compositional style of the monastery, and perhaps of other "oral" modes.[20] For instance, by interweaving paraphrase with the usual allegory and moral exhortation, Arator spreads Acts 10:9-16 over fifty lines (1.878-930). In the middle of the day Peter went to the upper story of a building, the high place teaching him to seek heavenly and not earthly things. It was the sixth hour, and Peter was hungry. Now, in the Sixth Age Christ entered a world created in six days. At the same hour that Peter hungered, Christ thirsted and sought water from the Samaritan woman (John 4:6). Peter's duty is to nourish faith; his hunger is satisfied when faith nourishes others.

> Qui solvere nosti
> Excute, Petre, meae retinacula tarda loquelae
> Deque tuis epulis exhaustae porrige linguae. (1.896-98)
>
> [O Peter, you who know how to loose, strike off the restraining ropes from my speech, and from your banquet extend (sustenance) to my exhausted tongue.]

The heavens opened in a vision, and a vessel came down to Peter, who makes food for the Church from whatever he eats. The vessel had four sides: the Church extends to the four corners of the world. It contained all sorts of beasts and birds, which signify the virtues and vices of mankind. Thus when God instructed Peter to kill and eat, He was revealing that the gentiles are to be poured into the bowels of the Church through baptism.

> qui vertitur alter habetur;
> Denique Saulus obit, quia Paulus vivere coepit. (1.912-13)
> [He who is turned about is considered changed; Saul perished at length because Paul began to live.]

But Peter refused to eat common or unclean animals, and before the vessel was returned to heaven God spoke twice more, telling him not to call common what God has cleansed. (So Peter later interprets the vision to mean that he should not call any man common or unclean: Acts 10:28.) The Triune God spoke thrice to Peter. Arius and Sabellius fell from the faith by distorting the Trinity.[21] (Their errors are described. This, like the corresponding passage in the Ananias section, is one of Arator's few anachronistic exempla, aside from references to other parts of the Bible.)[22] But the threefold command indicates One in Three, and the gentiles are called. All things are cleansed by the blood and water that flowed from Christ's side.

As stated before, the narrative is less important to Arator than the abstractions it occasions, and these presumably gratified medieval readers as much as the well-known story. But Arator did not ignore the relevance of Peter and Paul to his Roman audience, particularly those in attendance at S. Petrus ad Vincula. Peter's imprisonment (Acts 12:3-5) results in an apostrophe to the saint in which the anxiety of the poet's contemporaries is placed beside that of the Church praying for Peter's release (1.1016-18). And in the noble coda to the first book, Arator offers the Eternal City hope for relief from the Gothic War:

> His solidata fides, his est tibi, Roma, catenis
> Perpetuata salus; harum circumdata nexu
> Libera semper eris; quid enim non vincula praestent
> Quae tetigit qui cuncta potest absolvere? cuius
> Haec invicta manu vel religiosa triumpho
> Moenia non ullo penitus quatientur ab hoste.
> Claudit iter bellis qui portam pandit in astris.
> (1.1070-76)
> [For you, o Rome! faith has been made firm, salvation everlasting, by these chains (of Peter); enclosed in their

embrace, you will always be free; for what may the chains not furnish which he who can loosen all things has touched? By his power, these walls, unconquerable and even sacred in their triumph, will not be shaken deeply by any foe. He who opens the gate in heaven closes the way to wars.]

"How his hearers must have applauded the words!"[23]

Peter and Paul both cured lame men (Acts 3:1-11, 14:7-9), a fact which is allegorized into the salvation of the two peoples, Jews and gentiles; Peter's primacy is asserted (2.198 ff.). As a missionary to the gentiles Paul was a rapacious wolf—here a figure of Prudentius is reversed—

quid iam remanebit in orbe
Quod non ore trahas postquam solertia Graia
Cessit et invictas in dogmate vincis Athenas?
(2.486-88)
[for what will now remain in the world that you do not draw by your lips after Greek cleverness has ceased and you conquer an Athens unconquerable in doctrine?][24]

This is after his speech on the Areopagus, and Arator goes on to show how Paul supplies what Epicureans and Stoics lack (cf. Acts 17:18), adding a reminder of Paul's statement (which accidentally counters antique heroism) that he was what he was by the grace of God (1 Cor. 15:10).[25] The Hellenized Paul spoke effectively to the Greeks; Paul the Roman argued his citizenship against his being scourged without a trial (Acts 22:25 ff.). But his citizenship is absent from where it should have been recounted in Arator (2.973 ff.). It is saved for the later passage in which Paul makes his appeal (2.1051-66; cf. Acts 25:10-12), one that greatly condenses chapters 25 and 26 of Acts in order to hasten Paul on,

nimium ne gaudia nostra morentur (2.1051)
[lest our joys be too long delayed],

to his eventual arrival at "Latium."

meruitque venustas
Nominis occidui de lumine crescere verbi. (2.1065-66)
[And the beauty of the western (Roman) name deserved to increase from the light of the word.]

At first it might seem that Arator was most eager to get to chapter 27, which occupies the next section of his poem. The Bible describes a storm at sea and a shipwreck, favorite topics for rhetorical set pieces. Arator indulges for a while (2.1067 ff.), abundantly echoing such classical *loci* as the storm in *Aeneid* 1. But he refrains from an overlong display since he himself might be drowned by it. Paul at last is brought to his destination, and Arator greatly colors the city that Luke merely names:

> Venit ad excelsae sublimia culmina Romae. (2.1218; cf. Acts 28:14)
> [he came to the lofty pinnacles of exalted Rome.]

The finale of the poem (2.1219-50) skips the ending of Acts, the events following Paul's arrival (28:17-31). Arator meditates instead upon the martyrdom of Peter and Paul at Rome, where the two

> lumina . . . mundi (2.1219)
> [lights of the world]

(a phrase that Virgil had used for Bacchus and Ceres: *Georgics* 1.5-6) were joined. The City is personified, with a turreted crown as in Virgil and Lucan; she

> caput mundi circumtulit oris (2.1226)
> [surrounded her head with the regions of the world],

thus fulfilling the prophecy of Anchises, albeit the Empire is far different from the one envisaged by Aeneas' father.[26] She has united with the two apostles: Peter, the *princeps* of the Church, and Paul, who, as teacher of the gentiles, could not have come to a more appropriate place. This gathering indicates the primacy of Rome, and whatever Paul thunders there,

> Urbis cogit honor, subiectus ut audiat orbis (2.1232)
> [the honor of the City compels the subject world to hear]—

very ancient wordplay.[27] The two have overcome Caesar's threats and taught divine law in the tyrant's own citadel, winners in the *agon*. As the Children of Israel were led by the brothers Moses and Aaron, so Peter and Paul, joined by brotherly love, delivered idolatrous Rome from bondage to Pharaoh (the devil) and saved it from Egypt (the world).

The story as told by Arator was one of many Christian alternatives to Hellenic heroism; and like Juvencus' epic Gospel harmony, it even had some influence on interpretation of the Bible, as Bede's praise indicates.[28] The heroes were now different, yet the manner in which poets presented them retained a great deal of the old style: one reason for the Muses' being persecuted so long was that they could not easily be disconnected from this form. By and large, writers of the new faith came to fulfill, not to destroy or even replace. The ancient conventions could be made to represent reality once more—to invoke God was not to engage in a rhetorical exercise. Moreover, in a broad sense, these writers were not outside the mainstream. Nearly always one is aware of the antique forms underlying the most Christian of poems, thanks to the classical training that persisted in the schools. Much of that training survived for several more centuries, and epics continued to be written. Juvencus and his engaging successor, Arator, are at the beginning of a long series of Biblical poetry that would grace later ages, a tradition that includes Caedmon and Cynewulf in the vernacular, not to mention Milton and Klopstock.[29] One might quarrel with Arator's style, but the subsequent history of his genre should make us more sympathetic to his colorful elaborations and the boldness of his experiment with that "excellent subject."

The Translation

McKinlay's text was used for the translation, though some readings which did not involve alteration of words were adopted from Hudson-Williams (*Ad Vigil.* 29-30; *De Actibus* 1.56-58, 352-53, 635-36; 2.102-04, 364-67, 377-79, 595-97, *capit.* 623/5), Waszink (2.287-89, 590), Blomgren (2.638, *Ad Parth.* 29-36, 86-88), and the *PL* edition (2.746).[30] And a few misprints were corrected (*De Actibus* 1.192 [trahis*?*], 786 [stri*n*guntur], 826 [tua*e*], 907 [ferarum*,*]; 2.115 [*r*esonare], 358 [fi*n*e], 646 [Paulus sentio; nam], 981 [nar*r*antis], *capit.* 1067/7 [come*de*bat]; *Ad Parth.* 88 [Ecclesia*e*]). We relied upon McKinlay's indices to settle grammatical questions, and we often used the medieval glosses in his apparatus to determine such things as pronoun reference.[31] The three epistles have brief prose headings, while *De Actibus* is divided into sections by prose arguments (*capitula*), all but the first beginning *De eo ubi* ("Concerning the occasion on which").[32] They are probably not part of Arator's text but have been retained because of their handiness for keeping the reader informed of Arator's location in Acts.

Notes to the translation were held to a minimum because we saw no need to duplicate all the information contained in McKinlay's apparatus. There one can find the countless classical, Biblical, and ecclesiastical echoes and borrowings, the sources, for instance, of Arator's number symbolism. (On a few occasions when they cannot be found there, they have been included in our documentation.) Apart from those which are explanatory, the notes generally refer only to matters not in Acts and not easily located, but all direct quotations from outside Acts are identified. For the most part the reader is sent to other places in the Bible, places which clarify many a dark passage in Arator and serve in lieu of a lengthy explanation in the note itself.

Arator's Latin presents many problems. It was thought necessary to provide a literal translation as a way at least to suggest the level of his style and the complexity of his sentences (some of which had to be broken up, however); also, those who wish can thus follow the Latin better. To flatten him into colloquial American would be to falsify him. On the other hand, a completely literal rendering would be unintelligible, largely because of his amazingly abstract telling and interpreting of the story. Though this has been toned down somewhat, the reader will profit from having the Bible at hand, and not only for Acts. Metaphors which seem awkward or bizarre to modern taste have not been tampered with; they formed part of the poem's attraction in the Middle Ages. The sudden and dream- like shifts in focus, from the story to allegory and back again, have in some cases been relieved by paragraphing—none of which is in the original. Generally, the similar shifts in tense are not retained. Now and then Arator will move from past to present to past, and since he sometimes means the interlude to be nothing more than the historical present—or else the demands of meter cause the shift—it was usually thought best to smooth things out.[33] But it must be remembered that Arator shared with his fellow writers of Biblical epic a sense that the Christian poet is cooperative with the Spirit in spreading the word within a timeless economy beyond our understanding, and that the deeds of such as Peter and Paul, acted out in a Providential continuum, are as much a part of our times as they were of theirs. When Arator moves to the present he often seems to indicate an intense awareness of the immediacy of Christ, Peter, and Paul.

Arator's diction is repetitious, and he favors words pertaining to the military (as befits his Christian soldiers) and to agriculture (as befits his own name). A favorite and oft-repeated theme is that of gift-giving. Normally *donum* and *munus* are rendered literally as "gift" or "reward," but the reader should be aware that they can mean "grace" (cf. *charisma*, a gift of grace). Frequent too are such Biblical catchwords as *via* (the "way" of and through Christ) and *vita* (the true or Christian or eternal "life").

Words inserted in brackets are mostly outright clarifications of the text; otherwise they involve things which are not obviously implied by Arator and which require interpretation; or they signal a place where, for example, we have had to rearrange the order of phrases. Many of these insertions can be accounted for by the glosses.

All Biblical references are to the Vulgate edition and the Douay-Rheims translation, whose language was used from time to time when the relevant Latin was identical with that of the text, especially in the *capitula*. The Acts of Peter may be found in *The Apocryphal New Testament*, trans. Montague R. James (London: Oxford University Press, 1924). *The Oxford Dictionary of the Christian Church*, ed. F. L. Cross and E. A. Livingstone, 2nd edn. (London: Oxford University Press, 1974), was helpful throughout, but especially for the definitions in Book 1, nn. 42, 76, and Book 2, n. 52. Richard A. Lanham, *A Handlist of Rhetorical Terms* (Berkeley and Los Angeles: University of California Press, 1968), was at times consulted when the glosses employed such terms (e.g., Book 2, n. 64). The titles in the notes to this Introduction will serve as a basic bibliography; they made many contributions to the translation, acknowledged and unacknowledged.

We are also indebted to Denise Reynolds and Gail Howe for preparing the typescript, to Jo Ann Robichaud, Karen Clagett, and John Anderson for help with proofreading, and to Professors Richard Toporoski (University of Toronto), Margaret Schatkin (Boston College), and John Fleming (Princeton University) for advice on the translation.

The word-processing of the text was supported by Boston College. In the final stages, invaluable help was provided by Dr. Carl A. Raschke of the American Academy of Religion, as well as by Dr. Conrad Cherry and Mr. Dennis Ford of Scholars Press.

Notes for the Introduction

[1]The title since Arntzen's 1769 edition (*PL* 68, 45-252); in the MSS it is called *Historia Apostolica*. (*PL* = J. P. Migne, ed., *Patrologiae Cursus Completus, Series Latina*, 221 vols. [Paris, 1844-64].) An earlier form of this Introduction appeared as "Arator: A Revaluation," *Classical Folia* 31 (1977): 64-77.

[2]Eleanor S. Duckett, *The Gateway to the Middle Ages: France and Britain* (1938; Ann Arbor: University of Michigan Press, 1961) 70; F. J. E. Raby, *A History of Christian-Latin Poetry from the Beginnings to the Close of the Middle Ages*, 2nd edn. (Oxford: Oxford University Press, 1953) 120.

[3]Text and translation in W. F. Bolton, *A History of Anglo-Latin*

Literature 597-1066, 1 vol. to date (Princeton: Princeton University Press, 1967) 108.

[4]To take England as an example, the use of *De Actibus* by two famous grandchildren of pagans is illustrated by Max Manitius, "Zu Aldhelm und Baeda," *Sitzungsberichte der kaiserlichen Akademie der Wissenschaften*, Philosophisch-Historischen Classe 112 (Vienna, 1886) 580, 623-24; and by Arthur P. McKinlay, ed., *Aratoris Subdiaconi De Actibus Apostolorum*, Corpus Scriptorum Ecclesiasticorum Latinorum 72 (Vienna: Hoelder-Pichler-Tempsky, 1951) xxvi-xxviii. Arator is in Alcuin's list of books at York ca. 780 (McKinlay xxxi). Other medieval citations are in McKinlay's *testimonia* (xxi ff.); Max Manitius, *Geschichte der lateinischen Literatur des Mittelalters*, 3 vols. (1911-31; Munich: Beck, 1959) 1: 166-67. See also Lawrence T. Martin, "The Influence of Arator in Anglo-Saxon England," *Proceedings of the PMR Conference* 7 (1982): 75-81; Michael Roberts, *Biblical Epic and Rhetorical Paraphrase in Late Antiquity* (Liverpool: Francis Cairns, 1985) 224-25. Arator was especially popular from the ninth through the twelfth centuries.

[5]Charles Witke, *Numen Litterarum: The Old and the New in Latin Poetry from Constantine to Gregory the Great* (Leiden and Cologne: Brill, 1971) 218-19; Raby 117-19. Other important studies include K. Thraede, "Arator," *Jahrbuch für Antike und Christentum* 4 (1961): 187-96; Thraede, "Epos," *Reallexikon für Antike und Christentum*, ed. Theodor Klauser, 5 (Stuttgart: Anton Hiersemann, 1962): 1024-26; M. Manitius, *Geschichte der christlich-lateinischen Poesie bis zur Mitte des 8. Jahrhunderts* (Stuttgart, 1891) 366-76, also his other *Geschichte* (cited in n. 4, above) 1: 162-67; Martin Schanz, Carl Hosius, and Gustav Krüger, *Geschichte der römischen Literatur bis zum Gesetzgebungswerk des Kaisers Justinian*, 4 vols. (1914-35; Munich: Beck, 1959) 4.2: 391-94; Reinhart Herzog, *Die Bibelepik der lateinischen Spätantike: Formgeschichte einer erbaulichen Gattung*, 2 vols. (Munich: Wilhelm Fink, 1975-) 1: liv (all published); Dieter Kartschoke, *Bibeldichtung: Studien zur Geschichte der epischen Bibelparaphrase von Juvencus bis Otfrid von Weissenburg* (Munich: Wilhelm Fink, 1975) 53-55, 72-75, 93-97; Jacques Fontaine, *Naissance de la poésie dans l'occident chrétien* (Paris: Études Augustiniennes, 1981) 260-64. These works, together with McKinlay's edition, supply an extensive bibliography, as does a lengthy essay which deserves special mention: François Chatillon, "Arator déclamateur antijuif," *Revue du Moyen Âge Latin* 19 (1963): 5-128, 197-216; 20 (1964): 185-225; 24 (1968): 9-22; 25-34 (1969-78): 11-18; 35 (1979): 9-20. Among a great many other things, he argues that the poem's anti-judaism caused the great response from hearers of all classes, for

the Arian Goths were close to the Jews in their opposition to the consubstantiality of the Son.

[6]See Witke 218-22.

[7]*Praefatio in Librum Job* (*PL* 28, 1140-41). Cf. Ernst R. Curtius, *European Literature and the Latin Middle Ages*, trans. Willard R. Trask (1948; New York and Evanston: Harper & Row, 1963) 447-48.

[8]Gregory's epistle to Leander, ch. 5, prefacing the *Moralia* (*PL* 75, 516); Bede, *De Arte Metrica* (*PL* 90, 170).

[9]Witke 222-23.

[10]Cf. Harald Hagendahl, *Latin Fathers and the Classics: A Study on the Apologists, Jerome and Other Christian Writers*, Acta Universitatis Gothoburgensis 64.2 (Göteborg: Elander, 1958) 388-89.

[11]Cf. Prudentius, *Dittochaeon* 180. Paul says that he will have an *agon* in Jerusalem (2.846); cf. 2.1235.

[12]Another good example is 2.861-65. In a similar figure Arator calls himself a *tiro* under the generalship (*duce*) of Pope Vigilius (*Ad Vigilium* 29).

[13]Raby 119.

[14]Cf. 2.688 ff., on Demetrius of Ephesus, the silversmith who worshipped Diana (Acts 19:23 ff.).

[15]See the analysis of the passage (2.443 ff.; Acts 17:16 ff.) in Witke 223-27.

[16]The importance of these ideas in other Christian writers is discussed by Witke 44-48, 75-76, 83; Curtius 235.

[17]M. P. O. Morford describes the characteristics of this genre in *The Poet Lucan: Studies in Rhetorical Epic* (New York: Barnes & Noble, 1967) 3-4, 87. His words apply as well to several of the Christian epics.

[18]Cf. *Aen.* 3.56-57 (on the king of Thrace); Horace, *Carm.* 3.16.17-18; Ovid, *Metamorphoses* 1.131 (on the age of iron); 1 Tim. 6:10.

[19]Cf. Sedulius, *Carm. Pasch.* 1.299 ff.

[20]See Jean Leclercq, O.S.B., *The Love of Learning and the Desire for God: A Study of Monastic Culture*, trans. Catharine Misrahi (New York: Fordham University Press, 1961) 91-93.

[21]Cf. Sedulius, *Carm. Pasch.* 1.322-23.

[22]Others are clerical celibacy (2.357 ff.) and an attack on the Donatists (2.604-18).

[23]Raby 119.

[24]Cf. Prudentius, *Dittochaeon* 189. Again, Arator has altered the situation at Athens: cf. Witke 226.

[25]Christianity's objection to the ancient claims of superhuman-

ity is described by Charles N. Cochrane, *Christianity and Classical Culture: A Study of Thought and Action from Augustus to Augustine*, rev. edn. (1944; Oxford: Oxford University Press, 1957) 113 et passim.

[26]*Aen.* 6.781-87. Cf. Lucan, *Phars.* 1.185 ff.; Sidonius, *Carm.* 5.14.

[27]Cf. Curtius 28.

[28]Jerome quotes Juvencus in *In Matthaeum* (*PL* 26, 26), his only citation from a Christian poet except for unfavorable reference to Proba's cento. See Hagendahl 212n5; Martin 77-78.

[29]See Curtius 241, 459; Roberts 180-81, 224-25; Richard J. Schrader, "Caedmon and the Monks, the *Beowulf*-poet, and Literary Continuity in the Early Middle Ages," *American Benedictine Review* 31 (1980): 39-69.

[30]A. Hudson-Williams, "Notes on the Text and Interpretation of Arator," *Vigiliae Christianae* 7 (1953): 89-97; J. H. Waszink, "Notes on the Interpretation of Arator," *Vigiliae Christianae* 8 (1954): 87-92; Sven Blomgren, "Ad Aratorem et Fortunatum Adnotationes," *Eranos: Acta Philologica Suecana* 72 (1974): 143-55. An important review of McKinlay, by Luitpold Wallach, appears in *Speculum* 29 (1954): 145-50.

[31]See Arthur P. McKinlay, "Latin Commentaries on Arator," *Scriptorium* 6 (1952): 151-56.

[32]See Arthur P. McKinlay, "Studies in Arator: I. The Manuscript Tradition of the Capitula and Tituli," *Harvard Studies in Classical Philology* 43 (1932): 123-66. Cf. his edition, pp. ix, 155; Hudson-Williams 91.

[33]Chatillon (19: 31n49, 203) has noted the effect of such shifts (in *Ad Vigilium* 4, *De Actibus* 1.7). Cf. Roberts 180.

The Epistles to Florianus and Vigilius

The Epistle to Florianus[1]

To the holy and venerable lord, spiritually learned in the grace of Christ, the Abbot Florianus, Arator the subdeacon gives greeting.

O Florianus, you who already bear in your name the flower of merit, product of ripe understanding—for though still a young man, you have given instruction to the old, from which life might win its way to heaven—run to the aid of my song and out of your indulgent goodwill extend a hand frequently to one whose feet are slipping. I have indeed written with impoverished language, but about exploits that are rich, and a [single] drop flows from the great mass of the sea.

Though you have mighty things in your thousand volumes of eloquent tomes, read also lesser ones, and, after the manner of Nature, which the Author of the universe established, let things high and low be united in your studies. The Earth herself, which engenders the tigers [and] which nourishes the lions, offers her bosom to the ants, to the bees. And if you consider how the Ruler distributes all things, the mild have received wits, the savage strength. And Valor itself, exhausted, forsakes continuous toil and seeks to have diverse duties. The soldier, accustomed to put his cuirass on his limbs, rejoices to approach the exercise ground unarmed. And those who conquer iron-clad ranks and battle lines strike unwarlike game beasts with their spears. Therefore, slowing your pace and leaving ancient volumes, devote some time to a work which a godly theme enhances.

The Epistle to Vigilius

To the holy, most blessed and apostolic lord, foremost of all priests in the entire world, Pope Vigilius, Arator the subdeacon gives greeting.

Perceiving the flames of wars from the shaken walls, I was once part of a people fearing [an army's] weapons. You come, o most holy Pope Vigilius, as our common liberty to loosen the bonds for the flock which had been shut in. By the ministry of their Shepherd the sheep are snatched from the swords, and as you reclaim us we are borne upon godly shoulders. It suffices thus to have escaped bodily danger, but a greater gain for me is the salvation of my soul. Abandoning the court, I enter the Church as a shipwrecked man; I leave the faithless sails of the worldly sea. I am brought over to the snow-white, storm-free sheepfolds of Peter, and now I enjoy the anchorage of a welcome land. He for whom there was a dry road in the midst of the waves has prepared for our canvas a bay in the coast.[2] If I should cease to give thanks, I shall be held accountable. The nine [lepers] caused displeasure through the service of one.[3]

There is a burning in my mind to celebrate the labors of those [Apostles] by whose voice faith obtains a path in the world. Therefore I shall sing in verses the Acts which Luke related, and following his account I shall speak true poetry. I shall disclose alternately what the letter makes known and whatever mystical sense is revealed in my heart. The power of poetry is not unknown in the Sacred Books; lyric feet formed the Psalter; they say that the Song of Songs, the sayings of Jeremiah, and also Job were composed in hexameters in the original language. Great Father, when I offer this gift of love to you, consider that I am paying the debts I owe to your merits. Under your generalship I am chosen as a new recruit; under your instruction I learn doctrines; if anything from my lips is pleasing, the glory will be the teacher's.

Notes for the Epistles to Florianus and Vigilius

[1]The identity of Abbot Florianus is disputed. Pope Vigilius (537-55) was much involved in the political and theological turmoil of his age. Shortly after receiving Arator's epic, with the dedicatory epistle, he became seriously embroiled with Justinian over a question of orthodoxy.

[2]13-14: "He" is Peter or Christ (Matt. 14:22 ff.).

[3]16: Luke 17:17.

On the Acts of the Apostles

On the Acts of the Apostles

Book I

In the name of the Father and of the Son and of the Holy Spirit, with the assistance of blessed lord Peter.
{1-20}

When Judea, polluted by the blood of its crime, had dared the unspeakable and had finished its work, and when the Creator of the universe had given on behalf of the human race that which He took without seed from human members, having condescended so that He might touch the depths of hell without leaving the heights of heaven, [then] daylight went down to the Shades [and] dissolved the darkness [which had been] damned by eternal night; the fleeing stars left heaven in the company of God; Nature, terror-struck by the cross of Christ, desired to suffer in like manner, and the power of death perished in its victory, for, overwhelmed by the weight of the triumph, it lost all rights by being too rapacious; and the divine power, uniting limbs again, stirred quickened corpses to motion; the sepulchers stood open to life, and the ashes of the godly had a new birth after the tomb. The third day dawned; the Majesty returned in flesh and brought back from the abode of shadows His gleaming splendor so that the original fatherland, long closed off, might be sought again by man the exile.[1] The Almighty Himself prepared the way and bade bodies to reign with Him after the grave; when the poisonous seed died, He returned His own seedlings to the flowering garden.[2]

Concerning the occasion on which our Lord Jesus Christ, working miracles after the Resurrection and eating in the sight of the Apostles, whom He commanded to preach unto the ends of the earth, was taken up from the Mount of Olives on the fortieth day by a cloud and was lifted into heaven; and the disciples, wondering after the angels' admonition, returned a Sabbath day's journey to Jerusalem, where Mary the mother of Jesus was. {21-68; Acts 1}

Now, by manifest miracles during forty days in their sight, the Lord confirmed the faith of those whom He bade to be His witnesses to the ends of the earth in its wide boundary. The wonders of creation could not conceal God. What proof could the Risen One give so surely as His eating? Human bodies demonstrate life by this means. About to go to heaven, He went forth to walk round[3] the grove of olives because by its sacred bud it is a place of light and peace; He wished to return [to heaven] from that place, from which the divine fragrance makes agreeable a gleaming person with signed forehead. Since chrism, from the name of Christ, cleanses inwardly those anointed from above, He who will return as victor was raised to the starry firmament and had with Him what He had taken on. A new procession of triumph! God has sought earth, man the stars. What thunder was given for Him from the direction of heaven, and how greatly the celestial choirs resounded in praise when the Ruler of Olympus carried up on high whatever He took upon Himself below, and entering heaven attended by the trophy of His flesh, He placed in the citadel of light the spoils snatched from the jaws of the black abyss and exalted earthly limbs! With what mercy He receives him on account of whom was His coming and His going![4]

A deep amazement seized the disciples, whom men bright with shimmering visage addressed. Let us now at last observe with rejoicing those things which are familiar to us and sound wondrous, and let us approve of the manner of His rule through the powers that are subject to Him: born of a virgin mother, rising again by treading upon death, seeking the scepter of heaven, He announces [such] deeds by these [angelic] servants. Nor do the elements cease to serve their Thunderer; in His honor as He comes, a star does service as a soldier, going before the Magi; a cloud waits upon Him in obedience as He goes. Therefore after they heard the angelic address, the band chosen for the harvest left the revered summit of the Mount of Olives; they sought by a swift path, with which it was possible to go a mile on their Sabbath, the well-known walls where Mary, the gateway of God, the virgin mother of her Creator, formed by her own Son, was sitting at a religious gathering. The second virgin put to flight the woes of Eve's crime; there is no harm done to the sex; she restored what the first took away. Let grief not raise up complaints or vex mourning hearts with groaning over the old law; the very wickednesses and crime rather cause delight at this bargain, and a better lot comes to the redeemed world from the fall. The person, not the nature [of a woman] caused ruin; in those days a pregnant woman [brought forth] peril, in these one grew great to bring forth God, [Eve] begetting mortal things and [Mary] bearing divine, she through whom the Mediator came forth into the world and carried actual flesh to the heavens.

Concerning the occasion on which blessed Peter explained about the traitor Judas, how, having hanged himself, he burst in the middle and his bowels poured forth, and {how} the Field of Blood was named, reminding them that, as David had foretold, another should be chosen; and from Joseph, surnamed the Just, and Matthias, Matthias was assigned to be twelfth. {69-118; Acts 1}

Foremost among the band of Apostles, Peter had been called from his small boat; the scaly throng were wont to be caught by this fisher; suddenly, seen from the shore as he drew [his nets], he himself deserved to be drawn; Christ's fishing deigned to seize a disciple who must stretch the nets which are to catch the human race; the hand which had borne the fishhook was transferred to the key, and he who was eager to shift the dripping booty from the depths of the sea to the shore and to fill the craft with spoils, now in another area draws from the better waves [of baptism], nor, pursuing his profits through the waters, does he forsake his profession; to him the Lamb entrusted the sheep which He saved by His passion, and He enlarges His flock throughout the whole world under this shepherd; the venerable one, [Peter,] supreme in this office, rises and, introducing the holy undertaking, says in the presence of many: "You know that the mad traitor [Judas] paid to himself the price of his wickedness; he himself trembled at the loathsomeness of his offense, binding his unexampled, guilty voice in his throat; he deserved to be killed in that part where his fault was, and, retracting his crime by such a judgment, he gave his limbs up to such madness [suicide] that the penalty due to the common enemy fixed his position in the midst of the air; hated by heaven and earth, he perished between the two; his burst bowels fell out, to be buried in no tomb, and his ashes, disappearing into thin air, fled from the world. Nor is this revenge on Judas empty; it denies funeral rites and comes thus as acceptable punishment for an unjust income: for, although he had lately bought fields with the price of his death, [and] although the purchased ground with the name of Blood, collocating tombs for foreign ashes, makes the earth fruitful by means of the graves, the impious one is denied the fertility of his own field, and is alone excluded from the lands which bear sepulchers, he whose cruel trumpet [voice] began the gory wickedness, the standard-bearer who, planting a kiss, by a sign of peace waged war as a wolf on the Lamb."

Now there is need for prayers, since prophetic words proclaim who is permitted to complete the number [of the Apostles].[5] Thereupon, praying mightily, they choose two: Joseph, surnamed the Just, and Matthias—a name, as they say, which means "God's small one" in the Hebrew language, and by calling [him, God] confirms him as humble. Oh, how different are human from heavenly judgments! He who was just according to the praise of men is surpassed by the merit of a small one.

Twelve constellations of the [stellar] choir shine and cast the brilliance of Olympus on the earth. I shall proceed also to say what achievement this light reveals: the world is divided by the regions of its four sides;[6] a threefold faith calls this [world to belief], [and] in its name [the world] is washed in the font; therefore, four taken together thrice makes up the whole figure which the twelvefold order possesses, and to the devout disciples, to whom this baptism is commanded, a mystic reason gave cause for making up again the former number.

Concerning the occasion on which the Holy Spirit, descending in fire, filled the whole house where the Apostles had gathered. In differing languages they soon spoke of the wonderful works of God, so that foreigners of all nations were astonished, as it were, at their own languages. Certain men said that they were full of new wine, although it was [but] the third hour of the day. [119-59; Acts 2]

The Holy Spirit, descending from the ethereal hall, illumined with splendor the place where the blessed pedigree of the nascent Church was; with fire as their teacher, a glow suffused their mouths, and from their flowing words came forth an abundant harvest of languages; no letter did its duty, no vein of genius dripped from the ear,[7] nor did wax imprint the notable sayings; faith alone was the teaching and the rich theme of the word given from heaven, a new source of speaking which comes in many forms and alone is sufficient for the speech of eloquent persons from the whole world.

Long ago after the old ark had overcome the waters of the sea, malicious men wished to extend their tower [of Babel] into heaven. In them, irreligious hearts divided the forms of their speech, and the good will in these arrogant confederates perished with their voice. At that time there was a confusion of language for a homogenous race; now there is one [language] for many since [that language] rejoices at the appearance of the coming Church, [a language that] will have harmonious sounds; and [the Church] brings about a return of eloquence in peace for the obedient [Apostles], and the humble order gathers again what arrogant men scattered.

A matter of greatest importance compels [me] not to keep silent long as to why it is that the fostering Spirit is given to *them* as flame, [but] at the River Jordan as a dove;[8] I shall fitly sing this [mystery], and I shall fulfill the promises owed[9] if [the Spirit] brings His gifts. These two signs are allegories that there should be simplicity, which very appropriately [this] bird loves,[10] [and] that, lest [this simplicity] be sluggish [and] grow lukewarm without the fire of doctrine, there should also be faith that has been kindled. There [in the Jordan] He appointed by means of the waters [that they be] of one mind; here [with fire] He bids that they teach with flaming words.[11] Love presses hard upon their minds; zeal burns in their words.

Also, the error that they are moved by new wine is, by allegorical reasoning, the truth; the intoxicating teaching of heaven has filled them from a fresh spring. New vessels have taken on new liquid and are not spoiled by the bitter [liquid] which filled the old vats,[12] [the new vessels] drinking in from the vine which, with Christ as the cultivator, gave a banquet in words [and] from which those waters that He transformed are red,[13] and He made the poor flavor of the [Old] Law boil in the books of the Church.

The third hour[14] became celebrated by the heavenly sayings: the one God has this number, a single Substance distinguished by three Persons; [a Substance] which many proofs demonstrate to us is also at the same time demonstrated by the hour.

Concerning the occasion on which blessed Peter, preaching on the incarnation, passion, and resurrection of Christ the Lord and how the pains of hell have been dispelled, warned them to depart from the wicked race of the Jews and to be baptized; and on the same day he baptized three thousand. [160-210; Acts 2]

But Peter first, who in walking was served by the water, wishing then to cast his nets for the salvation of men so that he might rejoice as a fisher to raise these throngs by means of the font, recounted the heavenly triumphs as the people marvelled: "God came to the western shores, born in the fleshly way, subject to the law for men; [though] outside of time, He took his beginning from a mother, nor thought it unworthy, powerful in majesty as He was, to take the form of an earthly body and, as Creator, to be part of mankind and to call us back to Himself at the cost of Himself after the gift of salvation and after so many sick men had been raised up as their feebleness was put to flight, when He had furthermore brought back to the light [of life] bodies wept over and dead and had restored to them the air of the upper world. Also, permitting Himself to suffer in accordance with the law of flesh born from the womb of a mother, He Himself preferred to die in order that the world might not lose life. But that which was born of a child-bearing virgin, that died. Innocent, He was hung from a tree, and the burden of the tree [of Adam] was removed. Thus the wound of the unrighteous [Adam] became the medicine of God. [Christ] gleamed among the frightened shades as He sought the dim kingdom; sorrows fled Him, shimmering with His own light, whom chaos could not darken; Hell then feared to be, and confining no one its punishment returned upon itself; the torturer grew sluggish from unaccustomed leisure; Tartarus groaned sadly because no chains rattled. What might Death do there, where the Ferryman of life was going? Almighty God, whom no boundary ever holds, raised Him after His sacred burial; we saw Jesus shining in His body, and we beheld Him returning to His heaven.

"But flee, o wretches, the deadly sins of a people in whom, with God's coming to banish the old injuries, the added wounds of sacrilegious crime developed. Why, o parricide Judea, do you involve your children through vows of blood?[15] Why, now that Christ's blood has been shed, do you, condemned, oppress these [children] along with yourself and hasten to bring forth as guilty those not yet created, and [why does] your tongue, murderer, strike at your future offspring?[16] Their birth later than the crime keeps the peril alive, and the children of misdeeds perish from being born; stricken by the voice of their parents, they come into the light already punished. If there is concern to bring to an end the growth of abundant evil, revive your dead people in the blessed waters; the one hope of having the debt of punishment remitted after the crime is to wish to be reborn."

The shepherd now increased his sheep; that day he washed no fewer than three thousand of the people in the river of the Lamb. This exercise of baptism after the commands of God came about for the first time to prove the authority which had been given; for, divided by an equal number, the threefold Power gathered this people. [The number] one thousand signifies that which has been perfected; thus then we reckon periods by centuries when we discuss the times of the world. Matter perfected once is triply joined, and the mystic sense of the number [one thousand] makes [it a military] column. It is the holy form of the new flock.[17]

Concerning the occasion on which after the coming of the Holy Spirit all things were {held in} common by them, and they dwelled together with one mind, praising the Lord highly and having favor among all the people. {211-43: Acts 2}

Meanwhile, grace spreads through all their senses, and good will rich in love harvests wealth; and, that the devout may come together in an alliance with a sure pledge, they release their property and bind together their hearts; in mutual affection their property is allowed to be without boundaries; new laws for the blessed ones flow from their generous hand, for whom divided resources are doubled with rich fruitfulness, and what they make common to themselves grows for all, and they who wish nothing to be private lay hold of the whole. From what source this righteous dealing flows or what the spring of this goodness is, I shall now begin to recount. Twice the fostering Spirit had been granted to the holy disciples: once it had been breathed upon them by the risen Christ; afterwards the eloquent fire sent from heaven brought the men unknown words.[18] Lest we devise in our vain effort something untried, come, fostering Spirit! Without You, You are never spoken of;[19] give the gifts of language, You who give languages as a gift.

These rewards, having been [twice] repeated, strengthen, I think, the righteous to cultivate the two commands written together on two tablets: "Filled with fervent love, love God with your soul." Again He says, "May your neighbor also be dear to you as you [are dear to yourself]."[20] This covenant holds all the law; the fostering Spirit, coming twice through the hearts [of the Apostles], makes it: first the Creator gave Him [the Spirit] on earth, that man might be loved; afterwards He sent Him from heaven, that humanity might burn [with love] for God. The first love is that which strongly loves the Lord; from it [there is] then a second which unites the race of mortals. But the later in number begins first; that which is prior follows, keeping company as the second. Thus the teaching explains: "Unless you love your brother," it says, "whom it is possible to see, you do not know how to love God, Whom you cannot see."[21] Therefore let close-bound concord grow warm with mutual desire, and let love for one's brother establish the Lord in the heart; let it be in itself the essence of a double friendship.

Concerning the occasion on which blessed Peter, with John, saw a man of forty years, lame from his mother's womb, sitting and begging at the Beautiful Gate of the temple; and saying that he had no riches, he took him by the hand {and} cured him with a word. {The lame man,} leaping up and running, entered with them into the temple and went into Solomon's Porch. {244-92; Acts 3}

There was a lame man whose first day gave him both the beginnings of his life and the devastation of his limbs; he spent eight *lustra*[22] with his coeval infirmity; accompanied by John, Peter said to him, "Look at us"; hope disappointed the greedy prayer [for alms], but when [hope] withholds [one thing], it has better things in store. How often things despaired of are helpful to burdened men, and prosperity, born from an inauspicious seed, concealing its joyful nearness by sorrowful beginnings, comes in answer to prayer! The needy man will rejoice to have acquired more from an empty hand; he himself, asking for gifts, has been given to himself. "I have here no vein of metal," [Peter] answered, "to pour forth wealth; I, though poor, will be rich to a sick man; go forth and away!" A powerful medicine sprang from the voice of the one who made the command, and [the beggar's] feet delighted in restored walking. Leaving his cradle of long duration the mature man trod the ground, and his old frame moved itself on new soles; his walking with nimble speed displayed all that his birth did not furnish; the certainty of the mighty deed was plain.

But also another matter discloses to us what this affair contains: the people called Israel takes its name from that man who had broken off the contest injured, having tried to wrestle with God.[23] He himself first had this grave bodily mark, [but] afterwards the lame {people of} Israel had it in a wound of their understanding; they, slipping through their crimes, sank more in the heart than in the body, and in those very days were lame for forty years, having been removed from the land of Egypt, {but} desiring Egypt and seeking after idols. The feeble man is laid at the Beautiful Gate; the wretch is not strong enough to go farther or to touch the threshold of the gate; his guilt denies him entrance. Who are those accustomed to carry Israel, lame in its heart, and who strive to bring it to the gate {called} beautiful, which signifies Jesus by its name?[24] Isaiah, Daniel, and those like them who proclaim with prophetic voice in obscure {words} the manifest miracles of Christ; and He who has the name of the gate thus Himself warns: "I am the gate for you; he who refuses to enter through Me will be a guilty thief."[25] The prophets are able to carry {the lame man} to the gate, speaking things that are to be seen {in the future} more than things viewed {in the past}; they are not able to carry {him} into the temple; this door is entrusted to Peter, who, bearing witness to Christ, teaches things experienced {and} does not speak of things to come. You will lie fallen forever, old lame man, unless you ask Peter, who drives out guilt {and} shuns the burden of gold—{Peter,} whom the Creator of the world told not to carry even a wallet for himself.[26] Ask for the gifts of salvation; do not pursue perishable wealth, which he who will be rich with the Lord ought to spurn. After the threshold of the temple, the Porch of Solomon, who is rightly called Peacemaker, holds him {the lame man}; in the reign of faith, who will always be Peacemaker in the world except Christ?[27] He protects all who please Him under the guidance of Peter, by whose leadership they stand up.

Concerning the occasion on which, when there were already five thousand believers, the Jews forbade them to preach this miracle done in the name of Christ. After blessed Peter answered, they were scorned and sent away. They were returned to the other Apostles because, on account of the people, {the Jews} were afraid to hold them. {293-334; Acts 4}

The glory of the Church was now growing by five thousand men in its snow-white column; Judea strove to prevent Him from being worshipped, Him from whose gift flowed what {Peter's} efficacious virtue granted, but Peter's love did not know how to abandon Christ. He said: "We shall not keep silent about Him through whose bounty comes salvation, who made good the unfinished work by right of Creator; and a part [of the lame man] which [my] commands renew restores his entire glory. This redeemer who grants that the dead might rise had restored the stricken limbs." Wrath moved [the Jews] to complete their wickedness and to bring sacrilegious slaughter upon saints deserving reverence. O ever rebellious ones! They saw the gifts, yet set violence in motion; but they left off what they had begun, so as not to harm those [Apostles] whom the crowd protected, [and] for whom there was testimony of the favor granted, as the lame man showed; and with this [miracle] they were lifting up their hearts. For this walking announced no trifling wonders to the people, [walking] which a crude old slave of the ground undertook, moreover, in accordance with no law of this age, [walking] with which [the man's essential] nature, that long lay idle, was itself astonished to be moved, and, lately strengthened, it now impressed with its own pace new footsteps, which had been foreign to it.

Nevertheless the perverse race still raged, and what [the Apostles] joyfully proclaimed it forbade to be spoken. Why do you so often fall, Judea? You pay [money] so that the resurrection of Christ might be hidden by stealth, but madly seek empty proofs in [the guards'] sleep;[28] in feeble spite you wish what you sense has been done by [His] power to be denied by deceit. When the Lord undertook to destroy hell, he bore away from there [the sepulcher] His flesh, taking spoil of death. As a victor from the citadel of the cross, he furnished radiant signs.[29] The sun falls down into darkness, you rebel in your black heart; the earth trembles when shaken from its place, you adhere more fixedly; the rocks crack, you remain hard. Now the tearing of the veil lays bare the mysteries of the temple which long were hidden. Your Light comes to us, with you night alone has remained; endless death presses upon [you], for whom life never rises again. O ancient scion, be joined with the new [plants] and inserted in the rinds,[30] lest you perish deprived of nourishment, without whose bounty you will be a parched fig tree because you never wish to bring fruit to the hand of Christ nor see how the engrafted wild-olive has flourished bearing olives, and a full cluster of grapes burgeons, throughout the nations, from thorns [gentiles]. The wrath of the Ax [Christ] menaces the worn-out roots, in order that you may go to ruin when cut down and not grow verdant from being transplanted.

Concerning the occasion on which, after blessed Peter and John returned from the miracle of the lame man and the threats of the Jews, all the Apostles gave thanks to God the Creator of the world from the beginning, recalling about Herod and Pilate, and asking that He might deign to work wonders through their hands; the place where they were standing was moved, and the Holy Spirit came. {335-82; Acts 4}

When the wonderful healing which came to pass in the old man's body {and which was} told to the disciples was evident, and they learned the threats of the haughty nation, they sang a hymn with these words: "You, o God, {are He} who makes all living things in their proper forms by a creative word, and who beholding them on high sees them beforehand, and who begets the shapes of things through their names; when they came to be, a word was their seed, nor did Nature, following Your command, delay their beginning; then the Breath[31] of Your mouth arched the firmament, it bound up the dry land, it poured forth the seas, and Your will alone bestowed the material of the labor. Lest His like image {man} should carry a degrading yoke, the Ruler of Olympus concealed Himself beneath a servile covering in order that the fury of the gentiles might complete what they had begun.[32]

"What guile in Herod when he set in motion grievous violence, committed for the death of infants! Wounds which scarcely would find room, wandering about on their small limbs, took them as they were snatched from the breast; and at the cruel tyrant's command it was a penalty to be born; his attack took away a life which its loser did not know was in existence. O strange circumstance of death, to enter upon life only to end it and to be able to die without knowing it, since the first and last day are one and the same!

"Who can recall with dry eye or with pause in groaning the crime of Pilate, which the elements lamented? By his judgment Christ was willing to substitute His limbs for the trials of the world, that {His} flesh might get rid of fleshly evil, and that the fierce Enemy, by whose contrivance the poisonous weapons streamed forth, might fail to obtain the lamentable expiation of the ancient war, now that a matching substance had overcome,[33] lest the burden of {Adam's} crime go forward longer through {his} offspring. The condemnation of the righteous One has become the setting free of the guilty. Enable the seeds of the word to be cultivated through

Your gifts, and may this band,[34] enjoying new-ploughed miracles, gather under Your fructifying grace handfuls from which You Yourself may make up the granaries of heaven and crown the faithful wheat as the darnel perishes."

Where the holy feet were gleaming, the earth with its heavy weight seemed to run together,[35] and soon the fostering Spirit shone upon them, and eloquence arose in their failing tongues. Their prayers were heard and were effectual. We human offspring are earthy matter, and man, by his name, shows that his parent is mire.[36] The power of the Apostles' words, which made those created from earth have faith, altered and set in motion the ground; but as to the fact that the one place leapt and was shaken more [than others], Scripture announced that beautiful [are the] feet which bring peace;[37] therefore the joyful earth was moved under the tread of them [the Apostles] to whom peace was given by the word of the holy Master; transported through them, it has gone out into all lands with its swift favor.

Concerning the occasion on which there was one heart and one mind in many thousands of men who were believers; selling their estates they brought the price to be expended on the poor and placed it before the feet of the Apostles. {383-416; Acts 4}

Behold in how many distinguished crowds there begins to be one heart, and the people obtain one mind. Who can doubt the mystery of the teaching that one God has three Persons, when thousands of the people gather with like mind, and the spirits of a thronging mass are as one man? This is the multitude which will carry the everlasting cross, and following its faithful Lord it disdains the fields [of earth] since it will possess heaven. Surely this is greater power, rather to acquire the Whole out of a part, and to weigh what is enduring against the causes of what is perishable, and to seek gain through loss.[38] Generous one, you do not do these things as a seller of property, but, ambitious man, as one who wishes to keep his privileges, and you abandon for a short time what you desire to be yours forever. Thus, to scatter the fields was [really] the desire not to be in want; for of what advantage is property which perishes even though it is guarded? Whoever loses it has it to greater advantage laid up in the citadel of heaven. Seek thence, creditor, the wealth of greater interest, and lay up treasures where they can suffer no loss;

there no misfortune wears away perpetual wealth; you will possess everlastingly what you cause the Lord to owe.

Now, learned reader, see the sacred divisions {of the allegory} and ponder to yourself with keen mind what you think the meaning is when the display of golden metal is placed before the feet, not given over to holy hands. They show that what they avoid touching ought to be forsaken, and they teach that the gold they put beneath the feet ought to be trampled upon; that from which earthly cares come to the heart is cast upon the entirely similar earth. Learn in what place your mind stands, greedy one: what you guard breathlessly, what you clutch at your guardpost, what you so often burn to see, into the embraces of which you return in every dream, the holy ones shudder to handle, nor do they at that time carry {gold} about even when {it} provides good works. How much evil they observe enduring in it, and gold, even though it brings gifts, is despised!

Concerning the occasion on which Ananias embezzled part of the price of his property with the knowledge of his wife; and they claimed that it had been sold at a smaller price; and on account of this they were punished for their falseness after blessed Peter told Ananias that he had not lied to men but to God, because he had deceived the Holy Spirit. {417-54; Acts 5}

Unlucky Ananias perished by a wound of sin, reckoned as a thief because of his deception. His impious wife fell, struck down by a like punishment, because from a single crime there comes into being a common wickedness whenever a criminal act already committed is made one's own by complicity. Was not this sentence the punishment of a greedy heart?[39] When finally will the love for gold cease? It always enflames hearts, the human race is captured by it, from this root every evil springs forth, ambition for it {gold} burns the more violently the more it grows, and added profits got by plunder stimulate hunger {for more}.

But inasmuch as a changed intention bears the crime of deceit, and when there is, moreover, confirmation of a promise, it is proper to stand firm and not wish to violate what was first {promised} by what follows; it is more just to preserve a permanent right than to withdraw it. The punishment of the two established a warning for all, lest anyone should call {back} gifts which a solemn promise requires him to owe. Reflect, you of true faith, and consider the words of Peter, which are bright with blessed teaching: "Whoever persuaded you to be deceitful?" And he concluded by judging: "You do not deceive men by saying such things, you liar to God." The teaching which condemns the wicked strengthens the holy.

There is abundant instruction from many books that the fostering Spirit is God; and yet the Faith takes arms on this account; to what purpose do we contend further? Who would doubt that Peter said, "You who rightly come to the waters, stand in this place"?[40] It is sufficient defense against the foes of the Church that the teaching declares: you bitter divider, fear the final judgment![41] Unlucky Arius,[42] who is the author of your crime and of your error, tumbled down with his bowels poured out, [though] falling more in his mind, and in dying bore a common death with Judas, who, hanging by his neck, died emptied of his entrails, nor does the punishment separate those [two] whom an equal fault bound together, who fashioned a wound on the honor of the majesty [of the Holy Trinity] by their mouth; the one betrayed, the other divided, [each] guilty by a sacrilegious voice. God, the Judge of the world, is in three Persons; in Him there is at the same time one Power. He took away from them [Judas and Arius] the images of His works [their bodies], created by His goodness; they did not consider the glory of the Artificer and in their error thought that [Christ], who created all things, was created.

Concerning the occasion on which, as blessed Peter went through the midst of all the sick who were brought from various places, and they lay on pallets, the shadow of his holy body healed them, so that they were cured of their infirmities and of demons. {455-514; Acts 5}

Report [of Peter] summoned people to hasten from every place toward the mystic signs of salvation and to bring on their own pallets those feeble from diseases; they placed them in that part of the city where Peter directed his footsteps. Oh, if a more eloquent flow of words might move my lips, and an untiring voice and expressive tongue might give a hundredfold sound in this praise [of Peter], how much more splendid would be the expression of my eloquence, to reveal each detail with diverse figures of speech, and not to confine grand deeds with undistinguished words! What was the look of things when, in a brief moment, throngs of diseases were overcome, and there flowed to all an unexpected salvation, which the shadow of light, pouring from his serene body, brought into being, and when, rescued from the danger of death, they raised up their heads! But they were not able to catch in their sight the author of their good [health], [they] from whom his lofty virtue concealed the help it provided, and the thing was obtained before there had been any hope for it, and the hidden medicine gave the secret rewards of life, and [the medicine] carried away the fever of a gasping body without the sick man's knowing it; [the sick man] who demonstrated that it [the medicine] had come did not know that it was present, and the power of the event grew though it lacked recognition; the image of his [Peter's] splendor, flying through everything and healing what was harmful by its touch, though illusive to the eyes remained among [Peter's] gifts; and it left beds filled by its benefits everywhere, and cast forth black foes from the senses and stripped limbs of their ghostly mist.

Go swiftly, Peter, and beat aside the anxieties of men by your constant visits; the medicine of salvation travels with you; add to your journey; there is swift hope for joy's sake that your feet have no delay; your path is life; if you hasten, even now no one lies [sick]; you are raising all bodies by the movements of your shadow; and the silent crowd, unaware of prayer, acquires this [joy of healing] which at the same time one man receives when he asks. [Therefore, healing came to all at the request of one.][43]

You whom awe at so great a deed excites, seek what inner meaning this matter bears, and after searching through the books, know that this glory is granted to Peter alone; or see what teachings lie hidden beneath this [surface] appearance, [teachings] which I shall try to indicate, and [see] if that ability is granted, so that a dry brook may set in motion great waves: again, miracles come from ancient causes; in all matters the nature of things is comprehended more surely [than by a shadow] when [that nature is] sensed in its own body; there follows that [visible shadow] which is poured from a distinct body, and the shadow does not set bounds to a solid figure, but nevertheless [the shadow] itself shows that the body precedes it. We dwell in the Church on earth, which, it is permitted none to have doubted, signifies a heavenly [Church]; but that is more truly [the Church] which, at rest above the stars, is called celestial and high. This [earthly Church], which is seen in the brief career of an uncertain world, is appointed as the way of life and in this [present] time directs to the eternal [Church] those whom it gathers, and to those found acceptable it is the road for going from here to heavenly things. Peter rules both armies, and for their lot he gives the stars to those squadrons led from here, as has been revealed by the words of God: "What you have loosed," He said, "and what you bind on earth thus remain bound or loosed in heaven."[44] This [Church] which we see cultivated on soil, therefore, will be a type; what the clouds carry is firm. Peter, ruling both, designs there the body and here the shadow, in order that those sick men whom he freed from vices and offenses might be led unharmed to it [the Church above], which endures in heaven [and] will receive the holy throngs cleansed by this [earthly Church].

Concerning the occasion on which all the Apostles were thrust into prison by the jealousy of the Jews, lest they preach; an angel led them out at night; in the morning they were found in the temple rather than in prison, even though the doors were shut and guards were posted in that very place. {515-51; Acts 5}

Meanwhile the leaders of the temple grieved with a devouring jealousy that the Church had grown, and lest farmers of the soul sow what they reaped in the heart, they sent them away to the place of the prison, in order that the growing harvest be deprived of hoes. An angel drawing near thrust back the shadowy scrolls of night, and suddenly the stars shone in the calm sky, and daylight, bursting out at an hour not its own, caused the holy men to go to the temple; but the useless watch remained at the unmoved hinge in the sealed cavern, and the closed prison standing with its gates in a surrounding retaining wall lay open an unobstructed path for the Apostles' advance, and a deceitful door mocked the sentinels.

O faith, which is never disregarded: to it is supplied what Nature denies; [here] the Almighty does not permit her to use her own laws; how often He Himself in turn orders that to be possible which she in her amazement strongly urges is not accustomed to happen. If anyone in addition considers Thomas, with his feeble heart, let him seek teaching from this: seeing that the closed door, being penetrated, admitted God then,[45] is it astonishing if [Christ], in the flesh, approaches a gate in this manner, [He] whom a virgin bore, whom the unviolated womb of His mother conceived? What reason, I ask, was there to take human flesh unless it was to resurrect it? Returning after that, He presents His side for a witness and teaches that the ashes of our body must be made new by the example of His own, proving they are His limbs by their wounds. Now, Didymus,[46] you learn what wickedness it was to have doubted whether the Creator carried out what you see to have been permitted you [also]; if there is eagerness to ponder what Christ says, this symbol does not lack a voice [to explain] why the holy men left this darkness [of prison]. Endowing them richly, He said that these are the ministers of light and that they shine in the whole house just like lamps set atop a stand;[47] no night holds back those whom the Light Himself calls a candle, who have merited the God who bears gifts and is a witness [to the question] by what law that place concealed in its caverns so many suns in the [Apostolic] order, [suns] by which [that place] had a chance to know the eternal light so that with the expulsion of error the world might conquer darkness.

Concerning the occasion on which seven deacons were ordained— among them Stephen was chosen—because the Apostles had said that it was fitting for them to devote themselves rather to the word of preaching than to waiting on tables for the people. {552-85; Acts 6}

The powers of the ministry appropriate to the holy altars were established in seven men, chosen from everywhere, whom it was decided to call Levites [deacons]. How gloriously the band[48] of the Church began to shine, so as to mix the cup of life and offer the water with the blood of the Lamb! The glory conferred by this number [seven] carries along with it sublime mysteries, which the dimensions of my [poetic] journey do not allow me to pursue further now, lest speaking more I be found to have said less. Let it be an object of concern to deacons to ponder their office, with which cloak[49] of glory it is proper for this choir [of Levites] to shine, [a choir] whom the mystic design consecrates in the number for which heavenly things offer a pattern. I shall keep to my promised limit.

The venerable gathering said to the world: "It is suitable for us all to strive after the food of the word rather than the food of the table." Oh, rich glory of the Apostles' speech, never to permit people to feel a famine of virtues! A distributed sum of money is wont to increase; the coin of language entrusted [to them] was displeasing when it remained alone. That passage shows that food for the mind is better for an uncultivated people than victuals spread through their limbs, and that the richness of the heavenly word nourishes a broadly skilled mind. For of what advantage are the foods of bodily nourishment when the soul is hungry?

It is right for its [the soul's] hunger always to be fed by the mouth, so that we might strive after that table at which reclines a

Guest with fruitful words who shines in the whiteness of His clothing, lest anyone who comes shamefully to that [table] with foul speech should be forced to leave the blessed couches;[50] may that food proceeding from the Bread of Heaven bear salvation; may the throat of the heart desire it, and may the inner man hasten to taste it with the full mouth of the spirit; lest, however, the circumstance [waiting on tables] forsaken [by the Apostles] be thought more lowly, the handling of it was entrusted to [seven] distinguished deacons, and that precious [service] possessed a heavenly number.

Concerning the occasion on which Saint Stephen, who was made the first martyr, was stoned by the Jews, for whom he still prayed that they might be forgiven. He said that looking up to the opened heavens he saw the Son of Man standing at the right hand of God. While his persecutors stoned him, they laid their garments at the feet of Saul. {586-623; Acts 6-7}

Stephen now shines forth, he who has the crown in the contest as first possessor of his name, concerning whom a word prophetic of the palm foretold what the occasion brought about.[51] O martyr, give rise to struggles which will cause happy deaths, wherein punishment is glory and to fall is a rising, and by slaughter is born immortality embracing the rewards of everlasting life. Lo, to have merited thus to die was the beginning of a blessed life without end.

Insane, rebellious Judea, you hurl stones against Stephen, you who will always be stony because of your hard crime. Then Christ takes him up; to Him he makes his way by blood, an exultant soldier, summoned through his sacred wounds, and desiring to hasten to his rewards as a victor by this road, having traversed the glory of the snowy path he goes to the summit of the King on high, and through so many stones is joined to the One Rock. What strange fury is this, second to no one in ferocity, not to wish to spare a good man! With whirling arms you hurl the driven stones; he makes prayers, nor does he reflect upon whence the unspeakable hail falls; at the moment of his propitious death he prays for the sinning people. Even if you take with you all the weapons and hurl heavy rocks and massive weights, he whom you crush will be victorious; in death he plants as a farmer an example from which may rise the vineyard of Christ, and festive banquet guests [martyrs] may crown the chalice of the Lord.

Having the light of his heart he sees the opened heavens, so that what Christ does may not be hidden. [Christ] rises before the martyr; he then sees Him standing, though our belief is wont rather to honor Him as seated; the very Flesh joined to the Thunderer does honor to Itself in Stephen; the General in His foreknowledge arms those whom He summons to gifts; lest anyone here should fight uncertainly, the Body is revealed in the citadel of God as a reward to its witness.

The savage men lay down their garments at the feet of Saul, what the Hebrew calls hell.[52] Both sides now decide to declare what they deserve from this [martyrdom] when the martyr seeks heaven, the executioners "hell." The first circumstance [of martyrdom] reveals and makes as an example what flows from this fountain to one engaged in such a struggle; thus Tartarus quickly comes upon those who commit murder, while heaven lies open for the dying.[53]

Concerning the occasion on which, when the Holy Spirit came upon those baptized in Samaria as blessed Peter and John laid their hands upon them, Simon, who had already been baptized, afterwards as a magician offered them money that he might be able to do this. He was confounded when Peter rebuked him because his heart was held fast in gall and bitterness.
{624-71; Acts 8}

Often Peter made John his companion because his purity was pleasing to the Church; then, together with him, seeking the vicinity of Samaria, he marked the sheep who had washed in the waters of baptism; the fostering Spirit was present with them and caused different languages to come forth. Simon the magician had been here, washed indeed in the font but not clean in his heart; the subsequent punishment revealed him to the world as ignorant of the faith;[54] he wished to liken the gifts of God to the gathering together of gold, and to bring back by means of coin what a merchant buys at a price. Seeing him attempting this, Peter said, "What madness has moved you to this, wretch? Namely that you think that what the grace of the Lord gives is something for sale; it is not gained by gold but by a [right] disposition [of mind]; nor is it permitted that corrupt money, which the man whose eyes are fixed on the earth loves, should earn heaven; surely there remains no peace for you in this lot, nor will you, defiled by your tricks, be able to come to these things, you who seek what does not belong to you, swollen as you are with the gall of a bitter heart; for the Spirit enters those halls of the mind which are bright with honesty."

From this response the light of sacred allegory is revealed: the craft once constructed in the times of Noah manifested an image of the Church; it alone received every species, and bearing the counterpart of baptism for those enclosed, it diverted the waters toward life while the wandering throng endured deadly storms. It washed at the same time the dove and the raven, but the harmony of their souls did not make both equal; a throat full of plunder drew this [raven] from its way, and desiring to feed on death it was not able to follow what pertains to life; the bird friendly to fruits of the earth returned and did not succumb as a shipwreck to any waters, fearing to be fed on death, and by its striving it gives an example of holy labor, with what great love a faith devoted more to work is maintained, and the olive was the pledge of its modest beak; love always has the fruit of peace in its mouth. Both flew in the billows from one, holy bosom, cleansed by the surrounding sea in the hold of the saving [ship]; but one was banished and perished for its failure to return; therefore, the washing wave does not suffice for salvation unless the dove which is brought to life in the waters be without gall.

This Simon had touched the wave of baptism, but he was a raven seeking his profits, which never merit a God who is wont to drive off the sellers from the threshold of the temple. Let us pursue better things! Peter summons [us] to these; he is called the son of the dove by the mouth of God,[55] and deservedly brought forth by this mother he raises on high the work of the Church; thanks to her offspring this mother has a name which the fostering Spirit chooses, [who] deigned to be seen in the appearance of the blameless bird.

Concerning the occasion on which an angel told Philip to go to meet the eunuch treasurer of the queen of Ethiopia, and so told he approached the chariot. The eunuch soon lifted him up [into the chariot]; he was reading Isaiah at the passage in which he prophesies about the nativity and passion of Christ. After [Philip] had preached to him the good news, he sought to be baptized with water [he] designated. [672-707; *Acts 8*]

An angel exhorts Philip, filled with virtue, to take the

southern road where a eunuch of the Ethiopians, who faithfully keeps the riches of the queen in her palace, is proceeding with his yoked horses; he flies with swift chariot seeking fixed joys and will prove himself worthy in that very car to cast away the wheels of error. O how great a stock of good you will harvest, you who come to receive the so very precious gift of washing, and you store up in your sterile body what you may reap as the better fruit! Bring [onto your chariot] Philip, what the Hebrew calls the heart of the mouth: he proves the glory of his soul by the witness of his name;[56] he rejoices to hear this master, because he teaches with the authority of a disciple; he himself will explain whom the words of the prophet [Isaiah] refer to, and since [Christ] has performed everything in the past in the place in which He will now be reborn, if you hear with belief, He will also be born unto you, and from that time you will be reborn unto Him. When water is seen, speedily the fertile faith of the eunuch begins to burn; immersed in the stream he lays down the burden of the serpent, and [Philip] hastens from the chariot, imitating Elias' journey.[57]

No trifling occasion of hidden allegory shines in the image of [the eunuch's] country: the Almighty gave full approval for Moses to unite the Ethiopian woman to himself in the bond of marriage;[58] Scriptures reveal that he later spoke with the Lord face to face. What is there astonishing if love for the Law began to grow at that time when [the Law] had been joined to the Church? Rather, the Song of Songs does not conceal the fact that the everlasting bride comes from that region: it calls her black and beautiful;[59] she comes from the south, which burns the Ethiopian soil, to praise her Peacemaker in the mouth of Solomon, by which name [Pacificus] what Christ possesses has long been signified.[60] Already what is owed to the world[61] sends [the eunuch] ahead as guardian of [the Church's] riches, by whose protection she might begin to bring forth her wealth. What better treasure is in her than the glory of the font? What richer gold than a wealthy faith in the heart? Finally, how rightly is her herald a eunuch! As [faith] proceeds, lust is driven off, and the chaste capture the heavenly kingdoms.

Concerning the occasion on which Saul, going to Damascus to lay waste the Church of Christ, was struck by a brightness from heaven. Hearing and recognizing Christ, he fell blinded and was thus for three days, and baptized by Ananias he received his sight. Scales fell from his eyes, and afterwards, sent out in a basket, he escaped the trap of the Jews. {708-53; Acts 9}

Saul, breathing out bitterness, prepares in his Jewish ferocity to wage war at Damascus, but the Lamb, against whom the wolf hastens to rage, will be loved. Happy is the fate of a headlong fall in which sin tumbles, and he learns by the fall of his body to stand on the step of his soul; when he closes his eyes he opens then his heart, and the Creator of heaven is recognized as the light departs. How much [this] darkness earns! After the loss of his eyesight he sees greater things; fostering faith gives a marvellous example to the ages. Ananias casts out his fury—o strange victory! He whom the Hebrew called Sheep [Ananias] subdues a rapacious wolf; God will be proclaimed to the world by this herald, and pulled from the shadows of the Law, under which he was blind, he will bring light into all lands, singing about the everlasting Sun. Do not cease, o Saul, to make this day known; that night is given to you filled with the light of many men, and you carry your darkness here [in your body] in order that you may be able to purge [the darkness] of the world.

Now I shall seek the lessons full of allegory more deeply, and I shall attempt to reveal the radiance covered by shadows: in that Saul passed three days in darkness, the measure of his own example makes him faithful, and finally the punishment which gives teaching shows that the Lord was constrained not to refuse further after three days to have risen above chaos; when [Saul] began thus to recover his sight—because from eyes [which had been] darkened there also fell heavy scales, which a snake is wont to have by nature—he was healthy in his reason. More cruel than the deaf adder, Judea always will pour forth poison from her mouth; the serpent of perfidious Synagogue hisses in its den. The Savior said to His disciples, "You will tread upon snakes in order that your actions may be purer among the heavenly servants."[62] Previously [Paul] cast away snake-like crime and strife, and now as a teacher he wages better battles; since he had risen above the wicked, he deserves to escape their ambush while the gates are closed; a basket, which is customarily woven with bulrushes and palms in turn, gives covering to Saul, in glory retaining an allegory of the Church, for there is always contained in it the bulrush, by the waters [of baptism], and the palm, by the crowns [of martyrdom]: the wave of baptism and the blood of martyrdom promote the Church; not long since, the food produced beneath the tooth began to swell the insides of seven baskets while the multitude was feeding;[63] Scripture truly proclaims *that* number of churches in the world[64] inasmuch as the Spirit is the working force thus present in them and virtue marks their names, although we, however, sing the praises of one Church in them all. Therefore the visible form [the basket] protects the man; he himself serves it as a soldier [and] as a vessel [of election][65] remaining in the Vessel [Christ], and with Him as General he escapes safely from the enemy, a commander who conquers for Him in all battles.

Concerning the occasion on which blessed Peter, coming to Lydda after he had visited the saints, cured Aeneas, a paralytic who had lain sick for eight years. He said to him, "Rise and make [your bed] for yourself"; and directly those who were there believed in the Lord. [754-800; Acts 9]

After Peter, always watchful in his keeping guard over the sheepfold which had been entrusted to him, had gone round about the saints in due order, seeing everything, he directed his steps through the country of Lydda, where, standing at the walls he saw that Aeneas was living upon dead limbs and that he was dying although his soul was not dying, its body slackened by helpless joints; "Arise, paralytic," he said; "Take up your bed and do not be slow to perform service, you who have long been carried." By the operation of this utterance he who had formerly been helpless in his muscles was drawn up sound. He was again fashioned as a man then, and the corpse of long duration raised up to life limbs which had been powerless; and lifting himself up, he left the tomb of his empty bed, which had been a place of death for the wretched man. All the people began to stand along that street, and to many there came a full healing because of the sickness of one man, and once the water [of baptism] had been touched, [the healing] soon drove out the infection of each one's particular disease, washing in the font souls made strong by another's strength.

I shall reveal what are the hidden matters of sacred allegory here, if he whose word restores bodies moves my heart within me: in that the duration of his sickness is stated as eight years, lying beneath the Old Law during this time he was rightly feeble from dead limbs; to be sure, those whose child becomes hurt [through circumcision] when the eighth day comes round always have ruinous wounds; {Peter} healed the troubled one in that respect, and he strengthened in the flowing waters {of baptism} what had long been mangled by the peril of the flesh, in order that the eighth year might set the sick man free from the wounds of a dead body: Christ had already sanctified the solemn work {baptism} by reappearing on the day {after the Resurrection} arriving with that number.[66] The custom of the times {circumcision} remains, but restored by a better purpose; from the one {circumcision} creep wounds, from the other {baptism} they are taken away {and} undone; in the first the Law applies punishments, in the second healing cleanses in the waters, and limbs which in former times had long been loosed by death are bound up by life.

Also, that paralytic lay inactive for the years designated by {this} number; to him the nearby moving {pool of} Siloe, alas, offered no waters.[67] Judea is a pool surrounded by porticoes; for she has for her prison five halls, having reached the boundary of the Law through the five books of Moses; surrounded by the circuit of {the Law}, she, being weak, sees the everlasting Jesus without His gift {faith}, suffering in her books; from here He snatches one man, {and} coming to him He takes away his sins. Everywhere, the world reveals this allegory fitly; from the time that {Christ}, freeing it from the Sabbath, led it to the font,[68] grace overcame the Law. Peter applies to the Church the teachings of the Master; by means of his hand in the world one paralytic leaps up,[69] and as faith steps forth the world casts off its chains.

Concerning the occasion on which blessed Peter, summoned from Lydda into Joppe, raised up the dead Tabitha, who was also called Dorcas, a giver of alms, and presented her to the widows and the poor who had without speaking shown by their clothes the deeds done by her hand. {801-45; Acts 9}

You also, Joppe, rich in praise, famous for heavenly wonders, we sing in our songs, where Tabitha poured forth riches that shall endure and by her work was always a mother to the needy; she is placed in the middle of a bier at the closing of her time of life, washed more by tears,[70] she who is to live after her death. The faith {of paupers} calls upon Peter; bearing the pledge of divine love so that he might never be lacking in mercy, he is at hand to provide what prayers seek. The poor and the crowds of widows stand before him as he goes to the mourning house, and they show him arms loaded down with their clothes, which the hands of Dorcas had woven and given to them. O what solace their burning grief implores! They do not express their feeling of devotion with a sad murmur, nor do they repeat from their mouths the evidence of supplications; by their attentions they wish to speak what her good deeds deserve and choose rejection of their own voices, lest the wounds of their hearts which make a way for tears should lie hidden [from Peter]. To have said nothing is an eloquent theme for one grieving, and their exceedingly resonant case pleads what the tongue leaves unspoken, nor is it idle in his ear when clamorous faith, by which Peter is approached, is knocking; he is accustomed to hear the thoughts of the mind; he quickly bids all to go out, and bending his knee he becomes closer to the ground; then, praying, his lofty eloquence, poured out to the Thunderer, soon flies all the more above the stars, where it enters by means of his own keys.

Say, worldly wisdom,[71] where are *your* laws in that power? You deny that things corrupted are returned to their [former] selves, you who [now] see life [return] from death! As Peter senses that the gifts of God are present, by means of which she who lies there wept over is to be returned to health, turning to her he says: "Arise, Tabitha." She who is called returns, and, brought back to the light, she marvels that she outlived herself; he immediately takes her and presents her, standing, to the rejoicing throngs. That hand which was bountiful to the poor has deserved to touch Peter's right hand; by means of it the returning life raises her other limbs, and since it is going to flow through the whole body, [life] enters that [hand of hers] which was the cause [of her rising].

If we are rightly inspired, the renewed day of her soul is clearly suitable for allegory, [a soul,] turned back to the voice of Peter, which the darkness of exceedingly ancient peril had pressed down: the life burdened previously in the bosom of the dark Law, rising just like a second [soul], stands up in the Church's presence, and the light of works, the companion of faith, drives away the shadows, a salvation which had not been promised by the voice of the Law, because grace undertakes to give gifts of eternal life to those reborn in the font.

Concerning the occasion on which the angel announced at the ninth hour to Cornelius the centurion that his alms and prayers were pleasing to the Lord, advising him to send [men] to blessed Peter to learn the faith; he sent three men to him; he was the first of the gentiles baptized [by Peter]. [846-77; Acts 10]

Cornelius, born of gentile stock, was highly respected in the city of Caesarea; his life, given over to godly works, sanctified him for the waters, and he, who did whatever faith was wont to perform in those washed by baptism, began to believe through his actions; for an angel, sent from the stars, drawing near to him said, "The wealth which you distribute, the words which you pray, stand [pleasing] in the sight of the highest Lord; that rewards for your virtue not be lacking, accept the certain Way when Peter comes here." Thus the glistening messenger implanted with his word the commands for eternal washings.

It was then the ninth hour; by this hour the threefold faith [in the Trinity] now goes forth the more surely: a single third [hour], [or] again the thrice threefold [hour], teaches this, and each third makes the holy number, and [each] third made threefold manifests it. This is the mighty ninth hour,[72] which restored eyes to the world as day came back after the darkness, when light born from the rays of the cross brought forth dawn, and this eternal splendor filled all men; for it is certain that the world is a place filled with people from whom abundant light has shone upon a cleansed world, after they were washed in baptism. That tenth [number] which gives all things is wont to follow this [ninth]; the Judge offers it to those who keep the Ten Commandments and does not permit the first to precede in payment those who come after.[73]

Oh would that the enterprise of our lives might direct its course to the wealth of this time, [wealth] to which came the harbinger [Cornelius] of the sacred font, and would that the human race might keep in mind this lesson, so that a believer's love might watch for the reward of things and take as an example him who provided [an example] by the waters he deserved!

Already Cornelius, receptive to faith, bids three men to go to Peter with an indication of his wish: thus the threefold confession of the life-begetting water will come, and through that very number [the confession] will be maintained on the shores of Europe and Asia and Libya [Africa].[74]

Concerning the occasion on which blessed Peter saw a vessel disclosed to him with all kinds of animals at the sixth hour of the day, when he was hungry in the upper story. When he said that he could not eat from it, he heard a voice {saying} that he should not call unclean or common what God had made clean; and this was done thrice. {878-930; Acts 10}

Peter proceeds to go to the high upper story as it is now the blazing middle of the day: the high place looking down upon the earth teaches Peter always to follow heavenly, not earthly things; the circuit of the sixth hour also discloses the [number of the] Age in which Christ came into the world to dispense the wealth of Him who saves; and the number, with respect to days, manifests the pattern by which He earlier established the world which the Redeemer, coming in this very Age, forbids to be crushed under the sway of sin; and finally it is said that these things also took place at the sixth [hour]; when the Master, weary from His journey [and] sitting at the mouth of the well, asks for a cup of water by means of the maid's vessel, He is about to provide His Church's rest everywhere from the font.[75] In the [same] hour that Peter was hungry, that godly Master thirsted, always loving to add to his gifts; He who increased the honor of [Peter's] name enabled him at the same time to nourish faith; the earth will rejoice, filled by this hunger [of Peter's] which, richer than any gift, flows deliciously and, as it brings eternal feasts, leaves no one empty. O Peter, you who know how to loose, strike off the restraining ropes from my speech, and from your banquet extend [sustenance] to my exhausted tongue.

Enjoying his office, the celestial Keeper of the Keys sees heaven opened; from there an image of a vessel is let down, so that there might be a vision on earth that all things can be taken by the body of Peter, who makes into food for the Church whatever he takes to be eaten. The vision is brought before him, let down by its four sides: it is one image of the Church, which rises from the four parts of the world and spreads the eloquence of the same number of heralds [Evangelists], keeping together every kind of bird and domestic beast, of wild animal and reptile: these [animals] are connected to humans on account of their merits and vices; it is therefore clear that the Creator bids the gentiles to be poured into the bowels of the Church, as He instructs [Peter], "Kill and eat, take away what they are and make them like yourself." He who is turned about is considered changed; Saul perished at length because Paul began to live.

"Far be it [from me]," Peter says—how great is the holy man's reverence for the Law—and though he is hungry he spurns the offered food. Thrice the voice of the Lord resounds; it is repeated for [our] salvation: the Father and the Son and the Holy Spirit do this together. Arius, contentious against this faith, fell by denying that the One is in three Persons; Sabellius[76] admitted the One, but [it is] the Father, he said, who then in turn is called Son and Holy Spirit, being the same, but so that the whole is the Father Himself; and what the One greatest contains in its threefold order the former divides and the latter abandons. Both lie vanquished; for the threefold command of the [Lord's] bidding indicates a single number in [three] Persons, with their own qualities, [and] by this command He calls the gentiles; to believe this is right, if we wish to believe perfectly.

You make all things clean, o Christ, with your blood, which flowed from the wound of your side, conjoined with separate waters; the abominable snake wanders about and groans that his poison is overcome by the waters.

Concerning the occasion on which Peter, wondering over the vision, received the envoys of Cornelius. Being summoned, he set out with them to Cornelius, whom he forbade to greet him at his feet; and when the Holy Spirit came down as the preaching had begun, {Peter} immediately baptized him together with his {household}. {931-65; Acts 10}

Peter, being summoned, learns what his vision is; he has the name deservedly: for in the Hebrew speech Peter means Recognizing; as a gift Christ allows him, by whose recognizing He is revealed, thus to be named. He goes down to see those [three men] whom the one who was seeking the waters had sent there. Peter is said to go down to the people as he comes and [to go to] a new nation [the gentiles] which had not yet known the water; lacking the sacred font, a part [of them] had assuredly been immersed [in hell]; the way [of the font] guides those moving toward the wealth of a better fatherland, on which route one who ceases to go forward does not enter where life calls [him]. About to give the kingdom of heaven, [Peter] hastens with these same companions of Cornelius to sanctify the house; he does not permit him [Cornelius] to throw himself at his feet with bent knee; accustomed to giving gifts freely, he prevents a gesture of respect. Hence you, a new world, raise your head, you who had been struck down by the tooth of your ancient parent, and the font gives back a birthday to you; born again, do not press down your necks with your own sins, now that they are free from another's.

As soon as Peter begins to speak the sublime dogmas and to unfold the mysteries of the eternal Christ, the noble-spirited men are struck with amazement, and following his words they find the way. What does a faith free from doubt not offer believers? Gifts are never slow for it, nor do divine things make delay; thereupon the fostering Spirit, granting them diverse tongues as a rich gift, fills the house in an unwonted manner; Peter celebrates baptism to cleanse in the waters those washed in the flames [of the Holy Spirit].

This passage, in which the fostering Spirit comes before the waters He sanctified, is without parallel; He is accustomed always to add such gifts and to make haste with the imposition of hands only for those reborn in the font;[77] He performs these things in turn, lest anyone think that [it] is one's own [doing] and that what He, who provides willingly, varies [here] comes by [one's own] merits; for the fostering Spirit brings rewards which know no measure, and, providing more than was hoped for, His grace surpasses what was desired.

Concerning the occasion on which, after Peter had returned to Jerusalem, an inquiry was made why he had preached to the gentiles. To them he recounted his vision, through which he showed that it was by divine command that the gentiles had been baptized. {966-1006; *Acts* 11}

Going away from there, Peter reaches the exalted city which holds the ensigns of the cross; all the people ask whence [comes] salvation to the gentiles; to them the teacher reveals everything, and in addition warns that it is never right for those things which come from the goodness of God to be withheld; it is an opinion worthy of the godly man's word in that it openly shows the sentinel's love, how he who endlessly keeps these gates wishes to open the heavenly kingdoms to all. Why, o throng, do you mar our joys with complaints? These [preachings] are not gifts new to Peter; they were confirmed by that many [three] commands before, at the time when Christ allowed him to enjoy the glory of his gracious name;[78] He appointed him to carry out the laws of His Church when, looking out from the shore and seeing two boats standing near, He wished to sail in the vessel of Peter, delivering His teachings.[79]

The Synagogue, indeed, remained dry on the land after the instruction of the Master appointed the Church to pursue the deep; she stood perfidiously on the land while faith was already sailing on the sea; indeed, its own nature remained attached to each vessel:

Judea called "the son of Joseph" Him to whom Peter said, "You, o Christ, are proven to be the Son of God."[80] This part [of the Jews] which fell pursuing earthly things was fixed to the fields;[81] [the part] which grew as it spoke divine things when there was a draft without any fish in the darkness, went forth upon the deep. For in the season of light, because Christ the Light was present, [Peter] robbed the serpent's salt seas, in order that the holy nets of the font might draw all men to the shore and they might be stolen from the jaw of the dark-blue depths. For the sea was the world, from whose flood Peter, drawing in his moist lines as the word went fishing, filled ships with larger holds, because the host was going to come from two peoples; and he then raised up the gentiles with the sea as his servant, and he revealed the Church in the full ship; in its peaceful anchorage it stored up what it caught by the word of the Lord, who before had said that there were other sheep which he should seek;[82] [Christ] truly prepared these whom now [Peter] rightly called; through them the clemency of Peter gathered human property in heavenly enclosures.

Places will not be lacking in their own fame. Peter, who captured all things, was born in the city of Bethsaida, which was called Home of Hunters by the Hebrew name. How truly he arrived from that [city] as the Church's hunter, who, passing through all [regions], surrounded the gentiles and gathered them to the nets of faith!

Concerning the occasion on which, while blessed Peter was guarded in prison, an angel entered by night and the dwellingplace shone brightly; and striking his side, [the angel] took him along to where the iron gate which leads to Jerusalem opened itself; and there, realizing the truth of his deliverance, he gave thanks to God. A girl, upon seeing him, announced the joyful [news]. [1007-76; Acts 12]

Peter is shut up in a dark prison, but not without light, nor can the shadows with their black mist conceal the day of the Church; that fearful thing makes his punishment common for all: the guarding of Peter is a universal penalty; but the Shepherd guides His own sheepfold, having saved *His* guard, whom a triple confession of love for the Lord enriched with honor;[83] having a name from the name of the rock, bearing foundations which will never suffer collapse, Peter carries eternal appellations.

O Peter, awaited by your people, and dear in every season and to us now, come! Go forth as well to all whom old anxiety now vexes!

Presently in the deep of night a gleaming angel bearing stars enters the workhouse accompanied by daylight; as the servant of heaven comes, the shadows of the prison flee; the darkness, driven out, perishes as the new morning star shines; the black shade is banished, and the transformed nocturnal twilight sees the sun. Sleep is in Peter's body amid the chains of the surrounding band of guards; but since a faith which knows not how to sleep is awake in him, the Canticles proclaim: "I sleep with wakeful heart."[84]

Learn joyfully the teachings of the allegory, you who have deserved to be reborn in the flowing font, and discern in your godly heart what meaning abides in Peter's sacred body: the angel himself shows this way of accessible virtue; touching his side, he strikes [him] in that part on which the beginning of the Church depends;[85] the messenger raises him by that [part] from which he knows [the Church] had sprung. Noah fastened the holy doors in the side of the ark after the animals had been shut in; from this there was salvation while the flood was laying waste [the earth]. Eve, engendered as the offspring of her sleeping husband's side, was brought forth having the name of life;[86] thus she would have the more truly remained [immortal] if sin had never been. After Christ, the mystic Adam, deigned to give His limbs to the cross and to be oppressed by death in His slain flesh, whereby life returns, He consecrated new gifts of liquid through the path of His side.

Now the angel calls Peter by that part, so that every mind might believe that the glory of the Church depends upon him and might keep the faith, considering this celestial champion by whose bidding these feet deserve shoes, [these] which the Master's right hand touched, [and] it cleansed him wholly in the waters.[87] As they go forward, the closed gates yield; [Peter] thinks that everything is being done in deluding sleep, [but] the Majesty which knows no deceit has prepared true rewards for him; now the iron gate stands unobstructed by its bolt; the rigid doors relax their chains. Taking away from the gentiles the sharpness of their harsh savagery, [Peter] subdues all hard things, so that no fixed gate might bar the path on which the journey of the world will take place. Say, pride of the world,[88] why it is a thing of wonder if iron gates yield to Peter! God appoints him as the guard of the heavenly hall, and committing him to hold the summit of His Church, He orders him to overcome hell.

Straightway, free from the enemy, he sings the praises of God's work; the first girl demonstrates that he has come back from the darkness because the grace of Christ allowed a similar thing to be: He Himself, rising [from the dead], approached the sight of women; the glory of His returning flesh spoke to the sex which His mother has; it is clear from this also that the Church, which must carry unrestrained gladness to every flock, recognized her prophet [Peter].

Who may express such things by speaking, or lift weighty matters with words? That exceedingly great dread [of the Christian community] which bound their icy limbs was the measure of their happiness; through every age the splendor of this pledge endures, and it takes on the likeness of a star; Peter sanctified it with his body, and the angel with his speech.

For you, o Rome! faith has been made firm, salvation everlasting, by these chains [of Peter]; enclosed in their embrace, you will always be free; for what may the chains not furnish which he who can loosen all things has touched? By his power, these walls, unconquerable and even sacred in their triumph, will not be shaken deeply by any foe. He who opens the gate in heaven closes the way to wars.

Notes for Book I

[1] 16: Literally, the exile mud (*limo*). See 1.374-75 and note 36 below.

[2] 1-20: This highly abstract opening refers to the consequences of the crucifixion. Christ descended to hell to free the just; there was darkness, the earth quaked, and the dead awoke (Matt. 27:45, 51-54). Christ returned, having made it possible for Adam's children to enter Paradise; there, it is promised, the saved will reign with Him (2 Tim. 2:12).

[3] 28: Or, to illuminate (*lustrare*).

[4] 35-42: Christ demonstrated His mercy (*pietas*) toward humanity by taking on human form, by harrowing hell, and by opening the way for those to follow.

[5] 103-04: Ps. 108:8; cf. Acts 1:20.

[6] 113: That is, by the four cardinal points of the compass.

[7] 124: A gloss reminds us that learning enters the mind through the ear.

[8] 140: Matt. 3:16.

[9] 141: See the Epistle to Vigilius, 19-23.

[10] 143: Cf. Matt. 10:16.

[11] 146: Literally, that they burn in the mouth as they teach.

[12] 150-52: Cf. Luke 5:37-38. The "old vats" are the Scribes and

Pharisees.

[13]154: John 2:1-11.

[14]156: The hour when the Holy Spirit came (Acts 2:15).

[15]191-92: Matt. 27:25.

[16]195: Literally, the route of nature.

[17]209-10: *Millenarius* pertained to the command of 1000 soldiers. *Grex* ("flock") also had the sense "military troop."

[18]223-24: John 20:22; Acts 1:2, 2:1-4.

[19]226: Cf. 2 Pet. 1:21; 2.578-81.

[20]230-31: Matt. 22:37-40.

[21]239-41: 1 John 4:20.

[22]246: That is, forty years.

[23]262-64: Gen. 32:24-28.

[24]274: Cf. Ps. 44:3.

[25]278-79: John 10:1.

[26]285-86: Luke 10:4.

[27]289-91: Solomon was understood to mean *pacificus*; cf. Luke 12:51, Matt. 5:9.

[28]314-16: Matt. 28:12-15.

[29]320ff.: Matt. 27:51-54.

[30]327: The grafting metaphor includes word-play in *condere libris*, which can also mean "enrolled in the books."

[31]342: *Spiritus*.

[32]347: Cf. Ps. 2:1; Acts 4:25.

[33]363: That is, Christ in the flesh had conquered the sin of human flesh.

[34]367: Or, hand (*manus*).

[35]370-71: That is, the earth trembled beneath them (Acts 4:31).

[36]374-75: *Homo* deriving from *humus*.

[37]378-79: Isaiah 52:7, Nah. 1:15, Rom. 10:15.

[38]393: Cf. Luke 17:33.

[39]421-22: Reading the lines as a question. Perhaps, as in the *PL* edition, *nam* should be read for *non*.

[40]440-41: Perhaps from a lost part of the Acts of Peter (McKinlay's note). A gloss adds to the quotation: "so that we might join the Holy Spirit with the Father and the Son."

[41]442-43: Any "divider" of the Trinity, like Arius.

[42]444: Arianism denied the divinity of Christ, maintaining instead that He was created from nothing by the Father.

[43]487: The line is an interpolation.

[44]507-09: Matt. 16:19.

[45]532-33: John 20:19.

[46]539: Thomas, "the Twin" (John 20:24).

[47]544-46: Matt. 5:14-16.

[48]555: *Manus*. Cf. 1.367 and note 34 above.

[49]561: Or, amice (*amictu*); see Ps. 103:1-2.

[50]578-80: Cf. Matt. 22:11-14

[51]586-88: A crown (in Greek, *stephanos*) is an attribute of martyrs.

[52]618: Word-play on *Sheol*.

[53]622: Reading *occīdo* for McKinlay's *occĭdo* (p. 315).

[54]630-31: Peter cast him out of Judea, according to the Acts of Peter.

[55]667-68: Matt. 16:17 (Bar-Jona).

[56]680-82: A scholiast explains this interpretation of "Philip" thus: whatever he had in his heart he manifested by his mouth (*PL* 68, 151).

[57]690: 4 Kings 2:11.

[58]692-93: Num. 12:1.

[59]697-98: Cant. 1:4-5.

[60]699-701: Cf. 1.289-91 and note 27 above.

[61]701: The Church which is to be (gloss).

[62]736-37: Luke 10:19.

[63]746: John 6:9-13, Matt. 15:36-37. Cf. the Ambrosian hymn "Illuminans Altissimus," 23-24 (*PL* 16, 1411).

[64]747-48: Apoc. 1:4, 1:11.

[65]752: Acts 9:15.

[66]781: John 20:26.

[67]787-89: John 9:1-11, 5:3-7.

[68]796-97: John 5:10.

[69]799: A reference to his apostolate to the Jews.

[70]805: Than by the usual laving of the dead (cf. Acts 9:37).

[71]826: The belief that the soul does not survive the body.

[72]860: When Christ died (Luke 23:44).

[73]866-68: Matt. 20:1-16. "Tenth" translates *denarius*.

[74]875-77: Through his sending three, the confession of faith in the Trinity on the three (gentile) continents is signified.

[75]886-90: John 4:6-14.

[76]919: The Sabellians, or Modalist Monarchians, held that the only differentiation of the Persons of the Trinity was a succession of modes or operations; the Father therefore suffered as the Son.

[77]959-61: Cf. Matt. 3:16.

[78]974-76: The threefold command (Acts 10:13-16) had been

anticipated by Christ's telling Peter thrice to feed His sheep (John 21:15-17), fulfilling His promise to make Peter the rock (*petra*) upon which He would build His Church (Matt. 16:18).

[79]977-79: Matt. 16:19, Luke 5:1-3.

[80]984-85: Matt. 14:33.

[81]985 ff.: Luke 5:2-7, John 21:3-11.

[82]998-99: John 10:16.

[83]1012-13: John 21:15-17.

[84]1027: Cant. 5:2.

[85]1032: A reference to the wound in Christ's side, mentioned below; its saving blood and water were the foundation of the Church (cf. 1.927-30).

[86]1037: Gen. 3:20.

[87]1045-46: John 13:5-9.

[88]1053: That is, worldly wisdom (cf. 1.826).

On the Acts of the Apostles

Book II

Concerning the occasion on which Saul, who is also Paul, being separated by the bidding of the Holy Spirit, came to Paphos, where {Sergius} Paulus was proconsul; and when a magician withstood him as he preached {and Paul} rebuked him so that he did not see the sun, immediately Paulus the proconsul believed. {1-39; Acts 13}

Forbidding the lamp lit by the shining word to glow under a bushel, the Spirit said, "Separate Saul for the work of preaching." Directly, that Peter for whom the word of the Master made all things possible consecrated him by the imposition of hands as [Paul] left. Departing Cyprus and Salamis, he continued on to Paphos, which, once given over to passions, is said to have remained a cave of sacrilegious lust and to have cultivated the fickle winged [gods] with shameless zeal.[1] From here the summit of his deeds arose, because a greater grace comes to failings; Paul was already an example to [Paphos] that sins could be remitted. What a glorious opportunity for praise was assigned to the man! He sowed pure beginnings in the region of luxury, and the wanton field increased its chaste fruits. After these things, to whom would virtue be unknown and difficult since it thus is seen to begin in a foul place, lest any barren region should be devoid of merits?

Yet an evil magician attempted to vie [with him] in eloquence; things always contrary to virtue made a way; the warrior of the Church, turning back the javelins, said, "Your deceit shows by what father you, his offspring, must perish; you will experience the nearness of death in your darkness, and for a time it is appointed [for you] not to see the sun and [not] to observe the shapes of things whose Maker you deny exists." Then clouds transformed his countenance with dark stains, and the color of his black heart came into his face; denied a path, he now asked for a guide that he might safely go, one whose steps he might follow closely in his walking, who might in pity give [him] aid; and through the empty air he felt the way of error. Paulus the proconsul soon learned that faith shone forth; for him the other's darkness was the cause of seeing.

Submissions to salvation, o Paul, are not strange [to you]; you well know that light rises from darkness. All these examples reveal a hidden allegory: if it is agreeable to touch upon secret things with a watchful mind, Paul, in his teaching, rightly undertook to perform miracles through the eyes, [he] from whom the radiance of his face flashed more greatly when the waxing day had been lost;[2] thus he was lately worthy to subdue the evil man and to conquer the enemy with the testimony of darkness: [though once] blind, he deserved to see forever.

Concerning the occasion on which Saint Paul, entering the synagogue at Antioch, called for silence with his hand; and there he preached at one and the same time about the exodus of the People of Israel out of Egypt through the sea and where different wonders were worked in the desert, and about the testimony of John the Baptist in what he maintained about Jesus. {40-95; Acts 13}

Paul visits the city named after Antiochus and immediately hastens to deliver words to the throngs which the synagogue holds, and asking for silence with his right hand, he says: "You know with what savagery the land of Egypt placed a yoke upon our fathers; God rescued them from [those] cruel fields through miracles, by which compliant Nature changed her course when the rod put the surface of the sea to flight, and the flood stood as an exile from its own shores, pleasing [the Jews] on account of the dusty path, and the power of the sea was subjected to serving feet; as the deep returned, [that power] was to make shipwreck for the guilty; commanded to change its laws by various means, it stretched out sand for these [Israelites], for these [Egyptians] it heaped up the waters: a road for the righteous, a wave for the guilty.

"When the rock struck [by Moses] gushed out watery pools from opened veins, having brought forth [and] bestowed a liquid stream from its dry summit, the ancient source did not display its nature, nor did it show its former custom as it bore new gifts; the everlasting law compelled it to follow what was not innate [in it], showing moreover that things different in origin could be produced [from each other], food from dew,[3] moisture from a sharp rock. For lest only a few wonders should flow from holy causes, stones poured forth water, and clouds overflowed [with] bread, and moisture from the air grew hard in solid food, and the ranks which long had empty throats were satisfied by fruitful waters, and the inhabitants of the cloud gave a feast, and [the Jews] devoured rain, and the shower was eaten.

"Thus the unconquerable hand, thus the fulsome grace of the Creator knows how to nourish the plaintive flocks and to place the sacred company in a better fatherland, so that the Fruit of the delightful womb might blossom unto the seeds of eternal life. For Christ has come, born of His mother Mary from the stock of David, He whom all the oracles of the prophets predict as coming after, God in the flesh and, creating Himself, entering a virgin's womb. Uncover whatever [the readings on] your Sabbaths conceal: you see clearly the teachings of their typical allegory shining forth in the folds of the holy Lamb; from His fire the old prophets drew their predictions, and He allowed [them] to say beforehand what afterward commenced to be. Mighty in virtue, John the Baptist proclaimed, 'I am not [He]; after me will come One the shoes of whose feet I am not worthy to touch, nor [am I worthy] to undo the tip of the lowly lace which binds lofty soles.' "[4]

How well did Paul's voice, mingling old with new, utter the principles of baptism! Nor does [his] Epistle cease in its teaching to repeat these things: "Our fathers shone from baptism in the Red Sea by the authority of Moses, through the Law, when at the same time the rock followed them as they journeyed; for the rock was Christ.[5] What, hard nation, do you still demand? Behold, in your books resounds, 'Be not slow in believing.'[6] Consider the miracles of the sea, which whispered the mystic gifts that were to come in the times of the cross, when Jesus stained the waters with His blood, and from one wound of His side flowed what should give the three gifts of life.[7] That redness of the sea was a situation [Christ's passion] which was to come: thus the Maker washed all men, thus He bought [them through His death]; this color of His payment is in the water of the sea, and in the shallows appear wonders owed to wood [the cross]."

Concerning the occasion on which Saint Paul again preached in the same synagogue about the passion of Christ and about His tomb and resurrection by the witness of David; and when the Jews kept him from speaking after some had believed, he said that he would preach to the gentiles; and those who were gentiles in that place believed. {96-155; Acts 13}

More than once Paul, burning to pour forth beams of light into darkened minds, recounted these words again in due order: "After Christ, clothed in a garment of flesh, performed the miracles of God everywhere, making manifest that He Himself had come as salvation for the world, the howling, godless throng, driven by the goads of madness, sought to have Him hung up and fastened to a cross by the power of Pilate: o offspring of the earth! What all your eager wishes could not obtain for you, the gifts of Christ, the bringer of salvation, have spontaneously vouchsafed; He came from the stars as the price of your liberty, restoring what was lost and raising what lay in tombs. See how you remain answerable to your own King; He Himself wished to die in order that you might not perish; yes, and after [those] sad deeds they wished to seal up the tomb, a guard being set for the purpose of a doubled crime, and to close the way of rising prepared for the Lord.

"O what blind wilfulness! It thinks that the eternal is bound by human law, and that He who raises other [bodies] so often cannot give back limbs to Himself after death. You remember what sounded from the voice of David's lyre: 'You will forbid your holy one to know corruption.'[8] Could He who remains Life bear delay in the dust of death, He whom God the Creator, enduring nothing of death, raises up? Death, having gone beyond the limit of its conquering, was finally conquered; when the Judge was touched, it gave up the accused at His command; robbed of its ancient spoils, it fell through its own warfare; and [Christ], coming to set free those who were bound, was not to be held back; the final duty of Avernus now began to die in the presence of Life, and [this duty], which before was subduing all things, then itself perished; and after the three days had passed, he went on the path of light that He had made, by which the whole of [human] nature rises again in its Lord. You see from the Law that deaths cannot be remitted;[9] seek Him by whose blood we, having been cleansed, are united with the kingdom of the Master, in whose party we already are by the pledge of the flesh which God was willing to bear."

Then these teachings [of Paul] gave some few men to the Church. [The Jews] forbade him to utter holy words any further. O ever empty, o barren Judea, you who shun seeds for fear that you should be able to bear fruit for yourself! To these [Jews] Paul said with his masterly speech: "It was proper for you, for you indeed, to know these things, but this light will be for others, since the Scriptures reveal: 'I have set you to be a light to the gentiles in the farthest places.' "[10] The gentile crowds were astonished, and seeking the font they wished to claim the distinction of the promised newness, and, begotten with water as a parent, they gained rebirth.

For so great a gift, I am led by the account in this passage to touch upon the trustworthiness of the story[11] which related that in those days when Rebecca was bearing two peoples and nations in her womb and enclosed their ranks in those narrow walls, and she consulted the Thunderer, asking with a prayerful heart, [she] merited the answer of God: "The first," He said, "remains the lesser and smaller among those [children] of yours, and the elder will be slave to the younger, and the younger will obtain the honor of the palm." The Church's conception produces all that the fruitful woman in labor carried in this womb, and the gathering of gentiles represents the second figure,[12] who grew in a womb in which he was the victor; [all of] which it is now necessary to remember and to proclaim with holy zeal, so that we might serve Him by whose good will it befell us to be called before being born, [Him] who offers us the gifts [of salvation] before the time [of birth].

Concerning the occasion on which Saint Paul at Lystra cured a man who had never walked, lame from his mother's womb, when he made known that he had the beginnings of faith; they wished to do sacrifice to him [Paul]; he spoke to them about their old superstitions [and] admonished them that they now ought to believe in Christ. [156-241; Acts 14]

And now directing his path into the Lycaonian country, Paul approached Lystra. There was then in this city a lame man, born with an accompanying affliction, not knowing from the womb how to direct his steps; part of the man who was sick in his limbs had begun to die when he was born. When he learned the teaching of Paul, by whose instruction godly minds aim at the stars, he straightway wished to pursue divine things. O lame man, well were you lying there, about to walk for the first time on these paths: you sought heaven by your understanding although you had not yet bestirred yourself on earth, and though denied feet, you were strong enough to proceed farther. Paul, having explored what he held in the depths of his heart and [this] faithful lame man's love now standing on the word of God, thus began clearly: "Rise swiftly, and set yourself upright on your feet!" The healing which was commanded followed, and the old man went forth on his new path, and with continual movement struck the ground everywhere, and trying to run through all places he often feared the road because he did not know it, an old man just now rising with his steps from a weakness of many years.

When the crowd saw this they cried out and called [Paul] a god and provided him with garlands in order that a victim, a wild bull, might go forth to be sacrificed. Paul tore his tunic at these things, quickly holding the men back with clear reasoning, thus: "Why, I ask, are you giving these sacrifices to us, who, it is evident, are oppressed by a frail body under the law of earth? The glory of religion was formerly impious, when their own craftsmen feared gods molded from metals, when they dedicated temples to gods cut away from rock. Then perhaps it was permissible to sacrifice blameless flocks, and to consult warm entrails and seek a [prophetic] word in the organs of a dying beast; now it should be pleasing to obey the eternal God, abandoning vain altars; He furnished the seeds of life and invested the fields with various crops; by His command the grain rises up with full ears from the dying seed and the pruned vine-branch brings forth, the more fruitfully, grapes generated in its wound; as He directs the heavens, rains follow upon clear weather [and] season upon season: when they return behind [each other's] backs as they fly along, the constancy of the wandering year abides. Learn now to acclaim the Son of a holy virgin as true God on earth, and do not bring ruinous prayers to a wool-bearing flock, you whom the One Lamb sets free; He ransoms a world washed in His blood."

The faith was taught by these words; but the curing of the [lame man's] body results in a double achievement, and one healing proclaims a two-fold allegory, because in all the sea of the world there are two peoples of the Church through the words of two men [Peter and Paul]; the catch from it makes two ships full. For the feet of lame men showed these [gifts of salvation] bestowed on the human race [to two groups] in their turn; with them an image common to both peoples stands erect, displaying each of several separate things. He whom Peter allowed to rise on his ancient feet was neighbor to the gate;[13] the circumcised nation came from that place; to it the Psalms, the Law, and the prophets foretold the day of Christ. He whom Paul lifted from the ground as he lay sick in a distant land had never sat by the sanctuary of the temple, because [Paul], having undertaken [to preach] to the gentiles, by his holy mouth began to reveal the footsteps of a firm mind to ignorant throngs and to heal a people from whom the ancient word of God had been hidden. Thus when each lame man hastened, he raised an entire nation, and the walk of an individual signaled the salvation of a race; this glory of the events brought it to pass that the order makes Paul second to Peter, [but Paul] remains a master-builder on those foundations.

Still, in order that we might recount the praiseworthy actions of the Creator toward all things, there are these two blind men who said together to the Lord as the crowds hurried everywhere, "O most good Son of David, grant that [this] heavy darkness would depart, grant that we may see the light which we have not known till now!"[14] Then that hand always friendly to healing brought a sudden beaming light, and the night left their eyes, and exiled day illumined their eyes,[15] and their returned sight feared the unexpected twilight.

It is clear that these are the two peoples whom the harmful nature of their race has blinded; the mercy of Jesus, when He engaged in His journey [in the world], when he wished Himself to have the life of flesh, with [His] light renewed and cleansed the image which their faults produced; and straightway an unimpaired figure shone forth, which deserved to see God:[16] the eyes are the noblest part joined to the head; Christ creates them as a gift, He who is the Head and Brightness of the universe. In their extremity the feet are the lowest part of all; the cure of an apostolic voice heals them on the road, since the feet which carry peace to all lands are called beautiful.[17] Light has sprung up in the darkness through the gifts of the Master. These [Apostles] to whom the fate of the word has been entrusted determine the course, so that the medicine ensuing from the goodness of Him who went before might flourish, and that gradually healing might pass through the whole world.

Concerning the occasion on which Saint Paul, after many disputes in preaching to the baptized Jews, endured the question whether {any} of the gentiles should be baptized before they were circumcised. Therefore, he took counsel at Jerusalem, and blessed Peter advised that this not be imposed upon the gentiles, to which all the Apostles acceded. {242-306; Acts 15}

Now Paul had overcome the raging anger of men;[18] [but] as the faith was sailing along, treachery from a Jewish cloud poured forth sudden storms, [saying] that it was not possible for washing [baptism] to be given to anyone first, before circumcision of the flesh came to [him] in accordance with the Law of God. O hard nation! Why do you call for stone and iron [knives] besides? This [circumcision was] the shadow of allegory; the visible form was not to remain; leave the appearance, which you now see in its reality; the enduring life has come forth [promised] from Christ's mouth,[19] and he commands all who come to be reborn in the font. Why should they cut their members and lose a part when they are able to save the whole? Do not ask the power of newness to be crushed by ancient custom and your eyes, turned aside, to be fixed backwards after a straighter way directs everyone and lights a world where the thorn bushes are cut down.[20]

Immediately after this unsettled dispute, Paul journeyed to places in the city where memorials of the cross shone forth, and he revisited the holy princes of the apostolic authority, in whose presence he set forth all those things which had been done. Peter, whose greatest care it is to increase the flocks committed to him, calling all to rich pastures under his leadership expressed these words aloud: "You see that the eternal God has fulfilled in us those things, recounted in ancient times, which the prophets foretold to people by their teaching lips; as Redeemer He preferred that salvation be for all and allowed no one to be set apart in the ransom by which life returns; He ordered me to show this way open to the gentiles; why should their wishes be delayed and hindered, or why should these hoary mysteries [circumcision] be mixed with the new light? No law prevents those whom grace makes clean from coming. Impatient faith is the cause of heavenly love; Christ adopts this [faith], He makes this His own; whoever will deserve to enjoy it is already circumcised and is rightly reborn in the waves [of baptism]."

They decided to follow their shepherd; therefore, it pleased his servants to go together and free the gentiles with godly writings: that this yoke does not remain upon them, but that they must be careful not to worship images, whose offerings will always have to be accursed; not to eat those things strangled in their blood, which are polluted; [and to be careful] that impure lust, more savage than an enemy, does not oppress those whom the light has made clean in baptism.

In order that the teachings of this allegory be more clearly apparent, and [to learn] why the prefiguration [circumcision] which had proceeded first has now departed, it is important to remember the beginning: God said: "Abraham, so that you may now establish My everlasting Covenant for yourself and your offspring in the flesh, willingly circumcise your foreskins with a knife and bind a heavenly compact."[21] Let us look into the secret power, let us see in that wound the Covenant of God, which, in His foreknowledge, He established as a Testament, in order that He might unite the fellowship of Olympus with earth; [Abraham's] servant, who first found Rebecca at the water flowing from the font of the Church, learned to swear to it [the Convenant].[22] That licentious place of the body where Abram was circumcised contains lust, and as the accessory of vice it lies under the law of nature; he who was himself to be father of the seed from which the salvation of the world sprang forth to life,[23] freed [himself] of what sin burdens; his lust's having been cut out guaranteed virginal conduct; for this offspring conceived the divine path [Mary]; from this [source] was holy Mary begotten unto a new birth; in this she was a mother, though knowing no husband, and the Son of God sprang forth from a virgin's womb, and the Mediator fullfilled [the role of] man in all respects, lifting up earthly things from here, offering heavenly ones from there. Therefore the old type passes away with the birth of Christ; this visible shape [of Christ] fashions every law anew, and, with the banishing of the knife, the kindling Spirit circumcises the heart in the waves [of baptism]. Let those who are made whole in the waters not insert wounds in their members.

Concerning the occasion on which Saint Paul was forbidden by the Holy Spirit to preach in Asia; passing by Mysia also, he went over to Macedonia because he had seen a certain Macedonian standing in a vision and asking [him] to deign rather to set out for Macedonia. [307-82; Acts 16]

Meanwhile Paul, not knowing how to free his leisure from cares, teaches in the world, and he cultivates all men with mattocks of the word and makes the harvest of faith become yellow as the frost of error flees; the fostering Spirit forbids him to offer this to Asia, nor is Mysia, rich in land, poor in fertile soil, able at that time to bear the seeds of this salvation. Indeed, a man of Macedonia seen in sleep says this: "Have mercy, we pray; consider the Illyrian coast worthy." Oh, how much does unforeseen grace provide! Suddenly those who already have an appointed time are consumed by love. Thus, night having been driven away, the man skilled in speaking turns aside his journey, and hungry Macedonia feeds upon the fruit of his discourse, and through the gifts of sleep it deserves to understand the tongue that brings salvation.

A frequent question resounds: "If the Almighty, filled with bountiful generosity, proclaims, 'I have not come to destroy mankind but rather to save it,'[24] what occasion brings it about that this is denied to some and given to others, though the rich mercy of Jesus wills that it come to the aid of everyone jointly?" There is at hand a sufficient supply of examples, and a reading [of the Gospel] teaches us the allegory in this complex question, concerning which I shall relate a few things. As Luke narrates the account,[25] a certain man from the multitude asked to go as companion to Christ, [but] He forbade him to go forth with Him; [yet] then He called a silent person of His own accord. The Master who cleanses deep within knows which hearts now bear the word [and] whom evil error is still blocking up inwardly, so that teaching may then serve its function when it comes safely, which He says [thus], "Let dogs not undertake to do violence to holy things, and let pigs, laden down with mire, not turn their contagion against pearls."[26]

There remains another difficult matter in the poem, but for those to whom all things have been revealed from an ancient fountain, it is easy to turn to the drops furnished by [my] simple mouth: the Book of Exodus mentions the vestments of the holy Chief Priest, in which clothing he is truly able to become bright and to fashion the habit of his office with brilliant refinement;[27] ornamented with purple and gold borders, he stands in the midst of the altars; among these splendors is recounted clothing of similar garment on the thigh, by which he may put a covering upon his private parts when going forth to the temple, and as priest may strive to approach the mysteries chastely with bound loins. The more ancient law established this [rule] and ordered then that those bound members which dark lust possesses should be covered when he hastens to sacrifice to God, but leaving [the members] freed for marriage after holy things, lest a more sparing use not endure for the work of progeny and [lest] love grow cold for the husband of an unfruitful marriage, at a time when the true offspring carrying on this sacrifice might never admit any men from another stock,[28] whereby the honor derived from the Holy of Holies endures by virtue of an ancient name, and descendants return to be consecrated throughout time.

In place of creating what must be supplied, the Church's fostering faith now commands her bishops to be chaste always,[29] and being prudent she seeks in every tribe those whom she may duly approve, nor will that succession be one of blood, but rather of merit. Yet that type, without which no old [Testament] writing exists, at length remains the better in this innovation, and it changes its role as it recurs with another meaning, lest perchance the priest choose to generate [faith] before he sees the flocks are receptive, and that, when their ardor and hunger for knowledge are keen, he may know [they are receptive] in order to open their mouths more widely, so that no one should depart hungry. For Paul also rather often said that offspring can be given from the seed of the word, by his mentioning "my little children."[30]

It is pleasing then for procreative eloquence to be subdued for a little while and for the teacher to control his eagerness, moderating the forces of his talent for a time and carrying them bound up, keeping holy things for the cleansed lest the profane wear them away underfoot as they are poured out. Divine law forbids us to complain on this account; let his punished lineage ascribe this to the sins of Adam; for what may a guilty offspring rightly seek for itself with the throat of [its] parents, unless that benign Creator should wish to remit what headstrong error bore on a corrupted birthday? The only way of salvation will be the goodwill of Him who spares [us]; His compassion always lacks stipulations; offering things He never owed, Christ in His goodness speeds up His gifts to some, and in His justice delays them to others.[31]

Concerning the occasion on which Saint Paul ordered the pythonical spirit to go out of a girl who was a diviner; she kept proclaiming that it ought to be believed of Paul that he was a servant of the most high God; for this reason he was beaten and sent to prison with Silas, where, as the earth quaked while they were singing psalms at night, the chains of all were loosed; and when the jailer had wished to kill himself, {Paul} restrained {him}; afterwards he baptised him with his {household}. {383- 442; Acts 16}

When the route of the learned man glorified the well-known walls of Philippi in the land of the Macedonians, a raving girl under the goad of a pythonic spirit said, "Know that Paul is the servant of the eternal God." True testimony was heard from a lying witness, and a faithless attestor had a faithful voice; but it was not offered as an honor that dread compelled her to speak, nor did a fear which knew no love please his spirit. Grieving that hearts were oppressed by the foul demon, and not wishing to allow the profane to disclose divine ways, Paul said, "Begone, and fear to try these things any further!" Not liking the commands, the Enemy was gone, and the evil possessor left an empty house, and the woman, healed from the peril which had fled, fell silent in her praise of the man; what she began she finished, and by her silence taught better that this is true.[32] She used to make profit for her masters from the gifts of the crowd; a raging madness, from which she was free, filled them [her masters], and they murmured in the ear of the shameless people that religions contrary to the Roman religion were being announced seditiously, and that strange rites were going out through the world and the old gods had fallen.

Then, after the body of Paul had been struck with countless clubs, the crowd swiftly gathered where the prison was; they shut him in its innermost parts along with Silas, [and] their feet, enclosed in hollow wood, were held by blessed chains. O happy place of misfortune! in which [those two] bright lights shone in place of darkness, where ancient night[33] allowed everlasting day to occur; transformed into a snow-white palace of the Church and now bringing the gifts of salvation to all, how rightly it was a "starting-place"![34] There was a rush in the whole city to be the first to seek the remade building, or to plant a kiss on the doorposts and be blessed by touching part of the bolt.

Nocturnal sleep had now begun to creep through weary bodies; the earth, simulating catastrophe, leaped up, shaken violently in its bowels; and the moving ground shifted, opening the chambers, and the ministering fury of the earth did service for those who were singing hymns. O invincible faith, how great you were revealed! When danger came, the punishment fled, and perils increased with a twofold fear, so that torments might destroy the place [of torment]. Shaking his limbs out of his high couch when he saw the empty caves of death, the trembling guard wished to bring his hand to his throat with drawn sword-point; but it was not permitted to him to die with Paul as witness, by whose consolation he found life again and merited to be freed from his own prison; and going down to his house [the guard] provided poultices for the holy wounds, and, restored to himself, he who would soon touch heavenly water prepared a flowing wave; for Paul, loving to fix hearts on salvation, washed all of them together in a streaming river; life decreed that [the guard], to whom the grace of eternal light formerly revealed he was not to perish, later was reborn.

Once Eve, who was to deceive her husband, was caught by flattering words; now the [same] evil demon as then worked the mouth of a girl, and again seeking for crimes the sex of which he was a plunderer, he was a planner of sin by foretelling things to come to many people; but, enhancing the heavenly seal put on his image, the Apostle was now better than Adam, who had been a man of the earth[35] and believed things that were untrue. For what comes from the Enemy deceives, so that we all should be afraid to hear this abomination, and we should not be corrupted by the honey of bitter fraud, even if he who serves [us] falsehood utters the truth.

Concerning the occasion on which Saint Paul disputed with the Epicurean and Stoic philosophers at Athens, where he was called a babbler by the people; and afterwards he discoursed further before the magistrates, making mention of an altar which he had seen; and Dionysius the Areopagite believed first, with some others. {443-505; Acts 17}

Paul enters Athens, distinguished for genius and eloquence, and with the torrent of his oratory humbles a city filled with fierce contests; marvelling that he speaks in such a learned fashion, the crowd says, "From what shores does this sower of words proceed?" The people say without knowledge that Paul brings seeds, and speaking truth experience[36] an instructive error; for this fruitful wayfarer walks about on the earth and cultivates; his labor devotes itself to all, in order that the divine field might grow and the human soul, when cleansed, might yield fruit, lest what ought to bear crops appear worthless from its blades of darnel.

A zealous band impels him to accompany them to the chief men, to whom he speaks as he stands before them: "Sons of Cecrops,[37] whom the popular voice celebrates as flourishing with eloquent speech in your gymnasia, where deep love for sacrilegious novelty holds sway, we see that you have set up an altar 'to the unknown God,' who formed the stars, who gave the sea and the land, whom life has for a parent in order that we may be capable of motion, from whose fire we draw breath, whose image we are, of whom the poets have sung that from Him the human race has its being: [it is He] whom I preach: 'He has consecrated all things by his mouth.'[38] Why do you call divine these [idols] which you make, and think with empty fear that help which the earth brings forth is heavenly? The essence of metal lies lowest in the bowels of the earth; dug out from there it receives the aid of the talent which fashions it, whether there should come from it gods for the temples or pots for the hearth; the skill which has produced the gods is the cause of your fear; no one can shut in a Lord extended beyond all things and press Him together into small shapes; what is contained is smaller in size than [what] contains [it]. Your material [for creation] is in gold; the Artisan of the universe does not sustain the practice which they simulate, [they] whom He Himself created.

"What harsh crimes you will pay the penalty for! How foolish your wisdom will seem to you on the Day of Judgment when Christ will command all bodies to rise and the torments will be without end, and in order that it may torture the guilty, the fire preserves those whom it devours! Thus, flesh joined to God expiates fleshly actions, and the Avenger weighs personally the things committed by this [flesh] in which, as it died, He was willing to suffer; wishing to bring it to life after [descending to] Tartarus, He gave [it] to heaven, [Himself] immune from death." These [words] call many to the gifts [of grace]. Dionysius himself is the first in the citadel of that place to join new prizes to the honor [of Christ], and embracing the faith, he thus begins to be a wise man.

O Paul, you rapacious wolf! Jacob's benediction allowed you to have this name;[39] for what will now remain in the world that you do not draw by your lips after Greek cleverness has ceased and you conquer an Athens unconquerable in doctrine? Why do the Epicurean and the Stoic alone raise godless warfare? There is need to reveal on what grounds many flocks of sects have come together. Both [philosophies] choose to pursue the happy life, which the one esteems in the body, the other cultivates in the soul's virtue; the speech of Paul also gives rules for the godly life; thus, rather, on a united subject these [two philosophies] have opened their mouths with different words; the complete man exists combining the parts of body and soul, but now both [philosophies] want what neither has, following different things in their pursuits. A vessel [Paul] full of light subjects both [body and soul] to God, proclaiming, "I see how hostile the flesh is to my spirit,"[40] and again he begins wholesomely [to say] that what grace confers is not accomplished by one's own share [in the matter].[41] Let us frequent this road, because Christ is life and He Himself says that He is the way in order that we might advance to Him through Him;[42] and so that a holy lamp should not be wanting for our feet, a herald [Paul] given to the world announces the course of faith.

Concerning the occasion on which Saint Paul, coming to Corinth, found a man named Aquila preaching; he also remained with him, practising at the same time the trade of tentmaking, at which they were gifted (that is, the making of tabernacula); here Christ warned him not to cease preaching; and all in that place believed. {506-68; Acts 18}

Departing from Attica, Paul had left the people overcome by his holy speeches, and seeking the neighboring walls of Corinth, situated between two seas, he found a populous city which, though it touched the waves of an interchanging ocean, was thirsting for the everlasting waters; there that native of Pontus, Aquila, was at that time a teacher, a man having many testimonials of praise; Paul betook himself to his friendly lodgings, deigning to approach a household which was allied [to him] by love for his craft; for both were tentmakers, strong in zeal for their work and in teaching the Law. Christ said: "Now teach, Paul; no one hinders you while I am your companion; you see what a crowd there is for Me within those walls; press on in speaking; I strengthen your heart." These {words} advise that no one can ever complain about the slowness of a gift which Christ's mercy gives freely.

Lest by chance the allegory should lie hidden under ambiguity, I shall sing in what manner is granted [to me]: holy Scriptures often sang that arguments are drawn from a name and the greatest teachings [thence] arise. It is therefore of advantage to inquire more deeply who this dear host is, united with Paul {and} made a comrade in his trade, under the figure of what thing he was so named and with what kind of glory he is distinguished, pleasing in this respect also: Aquila's[43] faithful nature of its own accord acts out what the allegory holds; for an older bird, feeble from age and now with distorted vision, lies beneath the flame-spewing sun, and it warms its weighed-down feathers in the fire and opens its darkened eyes, and in order to return to the old daylight, it lets the burning rays into infirm eyes. Thus the weary bird takes the gifts of heat, from the fuel of which it receives strength and repairs the losses of old age; lest those be the only [gifts] which the fervid heat instills in it, it must be cleansed in the shallows of the waters; thrice it dives into the waves, and it puts off the weakness of age in the waters and raises from the font the youthful shape of beauty. What more evident act of religion will there be? When we are touched by the light of the true Sun,[44] we lose the contagions of an ancient age as faith draws near; then, reborn from our mother the water, we appear awkward in our newness; a restored infancy occurs again for an old man, and to those who live with a double birth, this is the better birthday.

[David,] whom the Spirit moved to work his excellent hand upon the harp, was well aware of this parable of the bird; he said, "You will be renewed in the fashion of an eagle;"[45] by this precept those proven good are allowed to feel that they are pleasing [to God] from the praise of [this] symbol, which the songs of the righteous affirm.[46]

Nor is Paul's trade, celebrated in [this] companion himself, without the excellence of hidden good; for he used to fashion strong tents as movable shelters on the road; the foreign traveller, going away anywhere farther off, sets these up, and he keeps out winters and sunny days with these hides. We also, driven from our first home through sin, are scattered by exile in the world; the way by which we may begin again our journey to the fatherland has finally been given back; o Paul, may there be protection for us in your camp, lest the storm of the world bring rains of sin and the fiery tempter emit the heat of wickedness; under such a covering, sure salvation sustains no attack of danger, nor does it fall prostrate [and] succumb to the might of the fierce Enemy. The leaders [Apostles] send forth mystic signs by the excellences of their trades: pursuing fish, Peter catches men; the guest of the sea remains in sacred waters. While Paul raises up earthly habitations, he teaches that he establishes heavenly ones, and having often built with his hand, he now constructs palaces with his word.

Concerning the occasion on which, when Saint Paul, in Ephesus, asked twelve men about the Holy Spirit, they said that they had not heard this name because they had been baptized by John; Paul taught them that the baptism of John had been in the name of the One who was to come; he baptized them with the baptism of Christ, and the Holy Spirit came upon them, immediately imparting various tongues. {569-622; Acts 19}

Coming to Ephesus, having traversed [these] territories seeking lands beyond, Paul teaches, and looking upon certain men who were there standing by, says as an inquirer, "Has the fostering Spirit come to these?" They say that they have long since been immersed in the font of John; for [they say] that till now they had been drawn along without any part in this Name; he washes them in the sacred river [of baptism], and the Holy Spirit immediately fills their mouths and gives them a shower of words with its accustomed power.

The profane too often set these weapons {words} in motion and prepare to fight according to their faction;[47] so that I might in speaking pour forth missiles against them, now, o fostering Spirit, moisten my mouth more copiously, that the teachings which You have given might be worthy of You! You road of speech, You path of language, You who are to speak, come, You who, through Your favors, always set in motion what we give back and {who always} recover {our} employment of Your gift!

John, a forerunner in the world, offered his baptism in the name of Him who was to come, and he himself prepared the way for the Lord, reminding everyone that there was afterwards going to be another baptism, which is given rightly {and} which the threefold Power is wont to illumine;[48] but because Christ chose rather to touch his waters, He made it the pattern for all to run to Him by the godly font, that henceforth the human race might not neglect the sacred wave which the Lord also had deigned {to touch} with His pure body when, as God was immersed through His servant, He washed the river. Now that the river had been touched, this work fell to the disciples, who Scripture proclaims had baptized many;[49] when there came {the baptism} of God, it was lawful for the baptism of His servant {John} to end ever since the foreteller had said these things earlier;[50] moreover, at the time Jesus brought about a complete baptism, as John had before,[51] why should He give that which was customary and proper {to John}? This example compelled Paul {to say} that {the Ephesians} ought to be reborn in the font of Christ.

By pointing his finger, John proclaimed the heavenly Lamb not as One who would come, but as One who had already come, announcing that He takes away the sins of the whole world. Why do you want to pretend that baptism is repeated, profane man?[52] Things which are different do not make a repetition; a repetition comprises the same matter, not another, and that selfsame thing which commenced to be the first time and {then} recurs would happen twice; for though the source {John's baptism} of the {sacrament's} beginning and the completion {Christ's baptism} which follows are different, each is said to be, and evidently is, {done} once, and no error burdens those things which, when compared, can be proved to be different. For all that, when anyone full of heretical darkness is stained by the lake of Avernus, {and} if he wishes to have the light of holy Church in the font, our faith does not compel him to go again to the wave because distorted teachings dragged him {to baptism} in the threefold Name; it is wont to investigate not who {they are} but rather what the imposed hands which taught him to confess the truth are able to give, and the error alone, which drags apart what the Spirit makes one, is banished.

The Scripture mentions also that these [Ephesians] were twice six. O sacred and happy quantity of the number! At the time when food had the right to spring from the seed of losses by the copious multitude, the glory of apostolic law was carried in that number of vessels.[53]

Concerning the occasion on which, when Saint Paul was in various ways imparting healing in Ephesus, seven Jews presumed to lay their hands on a demoniac, saying that they were doing this in the name of Christ, whom Paul preached; the demon, having given his answer in turn, drove them off with wounds; the people, seeing this, came to baptism. But some burned their books of magic, valued at fifty thousand pieces of silver. {623-87; Acts 19}

Now Paul, mighty in speech, had converted the city of Ephesus, and glory shone forth in heavenly miracles. And when distressed bodies faltered from countless diseases—nor had medicine employed by the hand of experts restored the wretched sick—they sought for themselves his sacred garments, being absent [from Paul]; burning faith was present in them [the sick] so that that heat [of theirs] would perish and a second flame would cause an end to their fever; in short, the aprons and handkerchiefs of Paul, publicly taken away [from him and] spread over their limbs, pressed out the fire of their sickness, and the diseases buried in their members dissolved down to nothing; a strength which cures all had been touched, and no households were without a gift which they took from the healing clothing. Under this very power the threatening storm of [unclean] spirits also fled into thin air like a useless piece of smoke, lest the lovely workmanship of the Creator, which, molded from the earth, acquired the likeness of His heavenly image and bears the appearance of its Maker as a pledge [of redemption], be polluted by its [unclean] guest and the smell of a robber infect the temple of His glory.

At this time seven men of the Jewish race attempted strange battles. Earlier they spoke thus: "That Jesus whom Paul preaches by name, Him we also in like manner declare to you; leave this place occupied [by you]." A voice replied, "Christ I know," it said, "[and] Paul; for it is permitted [me] to shun you as unknown [to Christ]." Learn, hostile race, your madness; the demon confesses that He, whom you deny has come, is reigning, and you will be refuted by this very [demon] at whose goading you are ruined, to whom it is not allowed to be pleasing with speech that inspires terror; the cause of God, which the law of love accompanies, forbids one to say contradictory things in prayer. This is the true faith. Then what a spectacle it was for the people, and what a triumphant crown came to be carried thence as the Lord conquered, when gnashing with a rabid roar the excellently harmful wrath of the demon towards his own burst open their garments and cut up their faces, and, overcome, they fled their perils and turned their naked backs in headlong terror! Why, fierce Judea, will you not now be fearful about your destruction, you who thus perish at the hands of your allied enemy, you for whom the instigator and the punisher of the crime is the same, lest he be banished by your judgment, who is at the same time guilty through your sin?

Immediately the report spread through the city, flying everywhere, that even the voice of the devil gave out that the highest power is God's. They rejoiced to meet together [and] enter into the sacred waters and to wash their old stains in the new font and to be bright in the holy springs from which a single age of innocence is given at the same time to all. But others built fires with their books of magic that they might deserve the waters, and by means of fire they fled the fire. It was an exceedingly lofty flame, the splendor of which flew above the air, and sparks such as these seek heaven. They also reckoned a value of fifty thousand pieces of silver for the books, since on this condition the wrong-doers deserved to cancel out their crime.

This is the cause of this figure: in the Law the sacred number absolves sins, as of old David in all the [fiftieth] Psalm washed away his offenses and put his debts to flight; again, when the fiftieth year of Jubilee arrived, what had been alienated from one's own land was returned to its former master; lost liberty was restored to those who had been forced into slavery; the creditor released evil debts; and the exiled man saw the ancient threshold of his fatherland.[54] Also the ark was fifty cubits in breadth; low in the waters and safe from the sea it worked salvation under the number of mercy, and being kept safe prospered through the power of this sparing breadth, because by the forging of His forgiveness Christ founded His spacious Church everywhere; begun thus in the waters [of baptism], it is extended most broadly on the land.[55]

Concerning the occasion on which Demetrius the silversmith, who made silver shrines of Diana, raised up an insurrection against Saint Paul at Ephesus. After his address the wrathful ran together to the theater, where the uproar of the madmen was of no avail. {688-752; Acts 19}

At Ephesus unlucky Demetrius used to put silver shrines in sacrilegious places by his art, being wont to perform his offerings with a greater reward for his Diana; seeing that all the memorials of the ancient madness were disappearing, he groaned and stirred up vain wrath with these words: "Does it not make you ashamed, comrades, that our Diana has fallen, whom the praise of the world has esteemed? What salvation is to be hoped for any longer by mortals, if the gods cannot be without end through the ages? What statues will [men] now be able to give to shrines, what incense to altar fires? The foreigner Paul terrifies them [the gods] and calls whatever we make in the name of the gods dumb metal; their religion departs from the city, and the rejected Penates[56] have sought flight. Alas for me! Already I see the holy places founded long ago about to collapse with a sudden fall, the sanctuary of the famous temple also being brought to ashes and ruin. What citadel do we take or what power do we grasp, [we whose] ability for work has been hindered and for whom it will be a crime to have made Diana? Carry on! The time has come. Our last struggle has everything on its side if it is desperate; the only way for the conquered to conquer is to dread nothing; a sure destiny of triumph is in store [for those who] have stirred their hands [to action] for the gods above. Rise up in arms, and may our weapons demand back this goddess whom our prayers acclaim!"

Moved by these words, the people roared, and with a common shout they called Diana great, and with headlong running they went seditiously into the obscene theater. In no other forum was it fitting for the wanton ones to discuss the cause and service of Diana; a foul space contained the business of a shameful meeting; but the mindless passion vanished as a wisp which slips from the eyes into empty air, and, when dispersed, retains no traces. O pitiable band! Why do you consider eternal [the one] whom you strive to serve? You are the witness that she is torn forth as a fugitive from her shrines. By what right do you tremble [and] grieve at her perishing and try to associate with heaven [an idol] whom you deny remains behind in the earth?

Now the arrangement of the allegory will have to be looked into, and it will have to be seen with its hiding places opened up: Demetrius is said to have set up, in his madness, shrines for the goddess from silver alone, though Nature has brought forth many [metals] from her ample bosom, by which metals he might fashion these things, as bronze is animated with flowing features and the hands of genius cause rocks to live. And if we go through in due order the books which speak holy things, we shall find a way, because Scripture compares gold to pure understanding [and] silver to cultivated speech.[57] For the Psalm, to be sure, says this; but you, o glorious Moses, mention this more profoundly when you recite these words to the people: "Bring gold and silver for the glory of the temples."[58] That interior [gold] which lies in the mind [is] not the hard metallic substance which is concealed in the heart, but more clearly it excites that [understanding] which Christ loves; the mind in which there is precious faith offers gold, and in like manner [the mind] for which the heart's good drums resound in the voice provides silver, so that both together might worship the Lord: understanding from the mind, lofty style from the speech; thus the teachings of the Law demand that this gold and silver be prepared for godly temples [minds]. The prophetic words teach us what the Apostle himself reveals, that we are temples if all sins withdraw [from us]. Salvation will be in the heart of a believer, confession in his voice.[59]

To the sacrilegious man there was only one thing [eloquence]: Demetrius, whose eloquence moved these minds, built temples from silver [alone], so that the rule demonstrates that the false gods are worshipped without the understanding as judge, and that this undertaking does not come from the best faculty of the heart; this part alone [eloquence] is assigned to him which, wanting in reason, sows mere speech from the mouth.

Concerning the occasion on which Saint Paul, preaching in Troas in an upper room until night, caused lamps to be kindled; and there Eutychus, a youth sleeping in a window, fell from the third story and was found dead on the ground; Paul lay upon him, saying that his life was in him; and the boy, being revived, was called back to the first story, where Paul was teaching. {753-825; Acts 20}

You also, o Troy, carrying your standards in our song, put

aside your claims to glory and add to your praises triumphs which shine forth for you more brightly from a true action than do those wars of yours which resound in ornate tragic poetry. While the tongue [of Paul], the servant of God, was spreading seeds fraught with salvation, he lengthened into the late night the hours which were making more day for souls; gleaming lamps flickered in order that the faithful might shine with the fire of the word. Eutychus, alone, banished from the wakeful ones keeping watch, entrusted to a window limbs sunk in heavy sleep. O rest wrongly won! O hearts always given over to sleep, unprotected by good! How great the disasters he lies open to, whom night alone guards and who never raises his troubled head to better things! He who allows [himself] to fall asleep from God does not know how to be wakeful for danger. Why do you seek the empty chaos of the window, young man, or why are you restful in that place where you will come to disaster? It is a matter harmful for well-being to seek high, hanging [places] and to wish to snatch furtive dreams on a steep couch; you were able to recline on a better resting-place, in the word of God and on the advice of Paul to desire the coming of Him whose name is the Door, accessible by the threshold of righteousness, through which the sheep raised by the font walk to life.[60] Seek this [door], all of you, if you are concerned to escape the ravening jaws and bloody bites of the wolf, by whose mouth the one who flees from the Shepherd will be torn; He calls forth His scattered lambs by their names, and He does not permit the flock redeemed by His own death to be captured again by the Enemy in his snare and by a wound from his bitter tooth.

The hall resounded with a mournful tumult; a pitying crowd hurried together with repeated groans to see the place which, sad from a painful death, will be made a source of happiness. Clinging to his [the youth's] breast, Paul said, "He lives"; life followed that word, and death fled, being banished. How much, o Christ, Your power, working in Your servants, accomplishes! You, having returned to heaven and equal to the Father in eternal majesty, govern the laws on high. But because Your flesh born from the body of a virgin mother plundered the kingdom of Avernus, and [because] You brought back living limbs from Your own tomb and released bonds so very like iron, proving that You were willing to die in that part in which You were born and rose again, a second light returns to others with You as its cause and given at the same time by Your example, You who compel Tartarus, long since conquered, to surrender also to Your chosen servants. Meanwhile the happy corpse rose from death, and safe and sound [the youth] was led by a better way through three stories to Paul, at the sight of whom the boy began to be innocent, now worthy of the honor of life since he had turned the path of death [toward life].

This glory of the deed teaches one to explain the reasons according to an ancient allegory: Noah's ark is described as supported by three stories, bringing forth examples of the Church; the place of the humans stood in the rank of first, and cattle occupied the position of second, the third portion being given over to wild creatures: all of which the ark, properly joined together, bore through the waves, as in the font of baptism there is now one salvation for all, but there cannot be only one rank for [people's] character; for Noah is said to have built nests in it, [and] the Hebrew [tongue] calls him Just and Rest, because in him is Christ, who justly divides fixed rewards for His own. Whoever is a lover of virtue, seeking high things, is joined to Noah; one lesser by his smaller character stands nearest below; the lowest portion, given over to wild beasts, holds the hollow of Tartarus. Therefore Eutychus, falling thus from the highest place, remained lost on the shores of hell, and empty of human reason he began to have the rank of wild creatures; after Paul lay upon his breast and his wisdom poured forth its speech, raising by his mouth a soul slain by the law of the flesh, [Eutychus] returned to the Lord from death, [all of] which [Paul's] Epistle proclaims: "You who are sleeping, now rise quickly!" and again it urges strongly, "And raise yourself, waking from death!"[61] Now the boy is worthy to stand upon the threefold heights, because he has learned from the threefold doctrine what is the substance of eternal life.

Concerning the occasion on which Saint Paul, after the ancients were called together from Asia, said farewell on the shore, speaking and advising many things, showing that he had preached to them for three uninterrupted years, saying that he was going to Jerusalem and was about to suffer many things and that they would see him no more, admonishing them to give alms; and then [after] praying on his knees, he departed from the weeping crowd; when he had given his kiss to them, he proceeded to the ship. [826-912; Acts 20]

And now Paul, after having passed through the outposts of the world, was about to go to Jerusalem, whither the Spirit often advised him to go; desiring to speak an everlasting farewell on the friendly shore, he summoned together holy ones from all parts, giving forth these words from his loving soul: "O beloved band, which campaigns with the weapons of Christ! O people sprung from God most high! You have remembered the teachings of my love and zeal; always I have resolutely endured the gentile ranks and the mad rages of the Jews, that I might give the rules of life and that the faith made known among the people might be concealed from no one. I shall always be unsoiled by your blood, nor must I as a debtor compensate for the buried money of a miserly mouth, and a barren field will not reproach [me] as unfruitful in the seed of the word; it is proper that you provide holy interest from it when the Maker will appear; He will be the examiner of merit and will demand back from His servants the increase of His measure.[62] I have been eager to bear seeds to the understanding; I have sown them far and wide, entrusting them to the furrows; but bad earth will grieve at its scanty harvest.

"I go to see the city of the cross, [a place] deserving to be venerated by the nations, whither [the Spirit's] commands summon me: there the struggle of a different contest in which to fight will be given to me, for he who will determine to complete his course will endure all things: to suffer for the everlasting King is the mildest share of the afflictions which my desires cherish and an opportunity [to enter] the Kingdom. Preserve, o ministers, the Church of Christ, which by His blood He made a reward for us in the world; let the servants labor to retain what the Lord gave by His death.

"Now you will not see my face and features any longer; observe more watchfully, I pray, the flocks committed [to you], because wolves gather at the sheepfold with greedy tooth; if a plunderer should go [away] with spoils, it is the guard's fault; what the thief takes is lost by the deceit of the lazy shepherd.

"But there will also be a bitterer foe within, and the discord which makes its wound under cover of [feigned] peace brings a graver evil; do not yield to hardship; rest is destructive of virtue, and negligent honor crowns no one in the stadium; for a brave man, his own glory will be a cause for toil, and it is the rare soldier [who comes] to his rewards [when] there has been only peace for him; victory gets its seed from an enemy; from this it is born.

"The Lord is able to make your young trees fruitful;[63] He causes [us] to come to His gifts through His gifts and Himself supplies what is helpful. I have not taken splendid treasures [from you] with fradulent extravagence by exchange of goods, nor have I taken gifts, seeking you yourselves rather than your [possessions];

you know me, how these hands have fed with my companions.[64] Make it a practice to bring forth your riches into the streets of light and to place the treasure of your works in the city of heaven; it will have been of no advantage to have sought gold from buried places if the miser hides what the earth used to conceal; what does not increase in the case of a poor man [first] lies in the earth and [then] is returned to a sightless cave by a [miser's] darkly sinning hand. Open your hearts, I beseech you, to the heavenly warnings, and let no one refuse to provide houses for the needy flock, where one receives Christ in the guest."[65]

After having spoken thus, he gave his kiss; while praying, he at the same time bent his knee upon the ground, and all of them, touched with grief, flowed with holy tears, and they deserved to follow the ship with their accompanying gaze far through the waves; and while their eyes strained through the interposed clouds, a way onto the sea was given to their [minds'] eyes, and the ship, taken off by the breezes, was still seen [inwardly], and it soothed their minds by its image, and their capacity for seeing increased with the goodwill of their hearts. But because [Paul] said, "Night and day for three years I gave these teachings for your salvation," an allegory is revealed by this reckoning [of his]: he who utters three doctrines of the Church rather often brings forth the historical and allegorical Book, proclaiming [also] a moral [sense].[66] For thus the six pots reddened with the new liquid out of the old Law took three measures apiece.[67] The ancient form of the perfect sacrifice commanded that one offer three loaves from the basket;[68] to these [mysteries] is added what Christ said to His disciples, that three loaves ought to be given to one asking when it was already night;[69] that night surely is the world, so that, if anyone here desires the food of the word, you should produce a banquet, you who are asked, and teach the willing one that the Father and the Son [and] the Holy Spirit are one God, and that a single Substance trebles the number. Nor do the holy commands proclaim this only once. [Christ] said, "Should anyone force you, demanding that you go on ahead one [mile], go with him another two miles."[70] Do these commands not seem to say: if anyone in error and without knowledge of the way asks your opinion, be eager to say what God is, proclaim the Father, willingly add that there exists the Son and the fostering Spirit, three in number but nevertheless one.

Hence empty Judea, which is called a barren tree,[71] did not bear fruit in the three years though waited for [by God],[72] because, refusing to explain its books with threefold signification, it did not know how to give gifts to Christ in the numbers of faith.

Concerning the occasion on which Saint Paul was held by the Jews in the temple at Jerusalem. The tribune rescued him from them when they wished to kill him, {and} he put two chains upon him. He {Paul} addressed {them} in Hebrew, {telling them} how he had been converted to the Lord; and when he said that He had ordered him to depart from there and preach to the gentiles, they shouted that he ought to be taken away, that he should not live; and they threw their clothes, and dust, into the air; and concerning the inquiry which was broken off because of opposition to his words. {913-91; Acts 21-22}

Paul had now begun to approach the noble temple of Solomon and to render his devotions according to the old Law. A band of Jews seized him, and with raging tumult they shouted that he was condemned to death, but the tribune rushed forth among armed men and ordered him to be fettered in two chains. Nevertheless the torments which lay harshly upon his constricted arms did not tie his mind, because Paul's Epistle, full of light, proclaims that the servants can be bound [but] the faith cannot be bound, and that the word is not allowed to be restrained by tortures.[73]

And on the very steps he took his stand [and] spoke to the people in the Hebrew language: "O men, brothers and fathers! You know that I came to these shores untaught; [then] I was devoted in love to every teaching of the Law; I now use you as witnesses: bearing your letters, I burned to punish with slaughter the Christ-worshipping flocks at Damascus and to ban this faith from the ends of the earth. But mortal things cannot contend with their Maker. A light which was to close my eyes came down from heaven, and because of that glittering fire the intensified daylight was hidden [from me], and misty darkness lay upon my eyes; at the proper time of this [darkness], the brilliance coming with my night increased for me. It is usual to discern the causes of an occurrence after the fact; I saw the shadows well, even then about to enjoy a new Sun. But also there lingered in my ears a call from the mouth of God; Christ shook me with terror by repetition of the name 'Saul' lest I should again dare as a standard-bearer to wage war against Him. With what right shall I deny Him at whose blow I fell; from his grace I, though prostrate, rose by a better path and mounted upwards, and I sought to gain on high the happy gifts of my downfall!

"Now, o citizens, too often have we taken up cruel weapons. That blessed group which uses [me] its enemy as a witness teaches nothing doubtful. Why is it still pleasing to be guilty? Shine forth from my darkness; faith granted sight to me from the waves of the font, and an image of death began to live in the waters." (Alas! Rocky earth is never fruitful from its own seeds, and they [the Jews] who allow the soil to be barren are [an object] of useless labor.) "Afterwards, Jesus, having at length appeared to me, said these things: 'Saul, prepare to go far, far away; leave behind this city; it will not believe in Our name through you; rather, sing the words of salvation to the gentiles.' "

Immediately the querulous ranks seized this remark; they threw off their clothes and, casting dust a long way, raged with empty fickleness, and the rabid mob resounded with conflicting noises, endangering Paul. O wicked Judea! When you wished to destroy the Author of life, you spoke in the same way; the choice was yours, whom you in your clamor wanted left behind, but from your bloody mouth you ill-advisedly demanded a woeful crime, and you celebrated the joys of Passover by choosing a thief, and you doubled your madness, being savage towards a holy Man, gentle towards a guilty one.

In every struggle you despoil yourself, and you set yourself free [from Christ's aid] when, harsher than [the torments] themselves, you heap torments upon Stephen, take off your garment, and now lack clothing, because the punishment of the first father is connected to you[74] and you carry in your body the burden of the old transgression, hostile to the glory of the font so that you might not be renewed in the waters. At the birth of his crime, Adam knew that he was naked, and from this the lessons of guilt were revealed to the wretched man; the recurring source of death enters you, in whom an anger replete with wickedness twice implants behavior which sin engenders.[75] Now the tribune, seeing violence blaze at these words, attached cruel chains to Paul and sent him into an unfriendly barracks to be tortured.

We will sing of a well-known difference of opinion in [its proper] place, how it is to be overcome: Paul, speaking of his deeds, says that his companions saw the light there some time ago, yet that they did not drink in the voice with their ears; but then, at the time when he fell blind, his companions are said also to have heard the voice.[76] Thus the work of the narrator varies. But there is no doubt that it is necessary for both [passages] to harmonize; for then [according to Luke] they are said to have heard, to have received the sound, now [in Paul's own words] undoubtedly *not* to have heard. This will be a simple way of explanation: the voice is justly denied to have spoken since it was indistinct, nor is a thing believed to be given by speech when a man receiving it does not store it up in his understanding; he is stimulated so little on account of his doubting ear, and ambiguous noise strikes only the air; they are said at the same time thus to have heard, thus not to have heard; the one standpoint is of noise, the other standpoint is of true speech, and a single circumstance bears and bears again a twofold meaning.

Concerning the occasion on which Saint Paul was tortured in the barracks and beaten by whips. Forty Jews swore together against him not to eat or drink before they had killed Paul as he was going to the tribune Lysias. After a relative of Paul had betrayed this {to Paul}, he was sent at night by the tribune to Caesarea, to Felix the Governor, where he pled his case with the Jews and their orator, and afterward before Festus, {Felix'} successor, from whom he appealed to Caesar; for Felix had had him kept bound for his successor. {992-1066; Acts 23-25}

The occasion bids me to unfold in verses the ranks of torment burning on Paul's body, and the grave violence of the punishments, but my tongue is fearful. Let us flee from this part, o Grief, and shrinking from so mournful a crime, let us suppress our eloquence, lest perchance the reader fill his eyes with tears and the page be moistened by copious drops.

But these things could not satisfy their bloodthirsty minds; they were afire with love for crime and wished to dip their sacrilegious hands in Paul's blood. What cruel vows for evil! Forty sons of insane lineage imposed [a vow] upon themselves not to take any food and drink until it was given from the slaughter [they] carried out; to prefer a banquet from this [bloodshed]. O pale semblance of a heart! Cups of gore are better for you, o Judea, than [cups] of the water [of baptism], and not wishing to come to any table, you hunger for wickedness and seek to have the hunger sated by the corpse of a righteous man.

Moses did not establish as a precedent these fasts completed by as many [forty] days, you will recall, as [the number of] weapons which you take up;[77] and you see that for that many years the secret ways lay open wherein food made from dew flowed from the rich cloud and dry land poured forth in turn the waters of the rock;[78] in this [number] our forefathers deserved to enjoy the divine goodness and to nourish their souls with gifts from above. In this same number you come to rage cruelly, and you bring together the defiled covenants of your band so that one death might make many guilty.

Lysias learned these things and [also] in what place they prepared calamity, because a relative of Paul made them known; he therefore the more swiftly instructed that his commands be privately concealed, and at night he cautiously anticipated the dark work and ordered a picked company to attend Paul with watchful respect. O honorable informer, you will not be without the glory due your merits, and you do well by betrayal, a thing which is rarely rewarded; nor does the constancy which you dread to maintain for wickedness harm you: resolution in crime will be a crime, and when the unjust are joined together for evil-doing, then the fault is good faith, which true honor adorns with praises at the time when the cause is holy.

Surrounded by armed men, Paul immediately went to Caesarea, whither the mob ran, supported by its orator who, obtaining the Governor's ear, spoke useless words. At last, Paul spoke thus in reply: "O excellent Governor, we have all known long since that you follow the teachings of Justice, and that she is the temperate companion of your counsels; this goodwill persuades [me] to have trust and not to speak doubtfully before such a judge. We have not violated the holy custom of the Law and the temple, nor have we disturbed the ears of the people with aimless speech. Coming from the cities of Asia, we began to perform offerings which always aim at a pure intention. Who, I ask, will be free if this activity makes a man culpable? I pronounce without fear—for faith does not know how to dread hazards—that what they dare to call a sect is the way of light and with its new features is not opposed to the ancient laws of our fathers; it is now lawful for all men to believe that bodies can henceforth rise from the graves, ever since Christ, who founded all things, brought back from there His own [body]."

Felix was astounded, having lost his name;[79] another's chains, [those] by whose hindrance Paul is bound, made him guilty, and [Paul] was kept for Governor Festus' year of office.

Here we leave [the account], lest our joys be too long delayed—come now, o Paul, to Latium!—[we leave] the struggles which were incited in the crowded forum [of Caesarea] and what great deceit of the Jews is reported to have flowed forth; for Paul said these things: "I challenge you at Caesar's throne; as a Roman I call upon the aid of Caesar." To him Festus [replied]: "You shall quickly go, as you wish, to behold the judgment seat of Augustus." Paul, escaping from danger [but] not under the goad of fear, avoided the burden of a trial; his heart was always anxious {for him} to die for the sake of a better life; but the Author of his service had already told His herald and witness formerly that he was to go to Rome. The mercy of Jesus gave draughts from His vessel {Paul} to all in the world who thirsted for a drink from faith, and it ordered all men to be moistened by {Paul's} copious speech, and the beauty of the western[80] name deserved to increase from the light of the word.

Concerning the occasion on which Saint Paul, sailing to Italy under military guard, in such a way that he even came upon the Syrtis quicksands and the equipment of the ship was shattered, endured a storm for fourteen days, so that they did not see either the sun or the stars, nor did they take food; afterwards, he exhorted them as they were despairing, because an angel had announced that they had been granted to him by the Lord, and he urged them to take bread as he himself was eating, and thus they came to the island of Malta; when the ship broke up there, they all were cast out unharmed. {1067-1155; Acts 27}

The wayfarer had sailed from the eastern shore, taking the help of the south wind, by whose breath the ship was dividing the sea with an increasingly joyful path and with the wings of the sail open. But what mildness have the tricks of the winds ever possessed? Immediately the calm of the sea was broken by the blasts of the south-east wind, and the feigned peace of the blue sea was aflame with swollen waves; the sea raged on all sides and, lifting up its mass from the angry abyss, refused a sure path to the dragged-about ship; raised to the heavens and thrown down, it was joined to the earth as a pursuer of land and sky. The band equipped for the ship lacked the resources of its propitious skill, and they lay aside courage in their cold fear, and sightless under the black cloud they saw shipwreck over and over again, and the image of death was revealed within the caverns of the deep.

On historical grounds I am called to traverse vast quicksands and pursue mangled halyards and the fragments of the rudder, but I do not commit so frail a tongue to the sea, and I will flee from trying too long the swift gales, lest perhaps a too violent wave drown the meager language for the singer. It is important to touch upon a few things; I shall try the safe beaches: the guiding stars were hidden from the wave-tossed ship, nor did the heavens shine forth beneath the clouds with the rays of the sun, and though the world duly passed through many days, on the sea it was a single night, in which time they indulged in no food. How great, alas, is the pain of fear, to forget the torment of hunger!

Often an evil event produces the seeds for good circumstances. The sailors and the cohort of soldiers would have despised the honor of so famous a man if the sea were calmer; at last he was freed from their custody, and those delivered from the savage ocean respected the one whom they realized was their harbor. That calamity brought it about that what Paul was should not be hidden and that the holy man should stand revealed, with the sea as advocate; though lights had been taken away, the elements labored to show the man, and in the midst of darkness radiant faith appeared; a laurel is appointed to the righteous as a result of the punishment which terror works, and enduring virtue increases in adversity; using trial as its evidence, it has a test in regard to its merit.

Finally Paul, standing, enlivened the souls {which he had} called together, {speaking} with godly words in this manner: "O faithful youth, would that you had earlier wished to obey our advice not to leave the shores of Crete {and} suffer the fury of the raging deep! You would not have endured the threats of sea and sky nor the woeful burden of devastating loss, nor would Well-being made desperate have groaned at the nearness of death in so great a storm. But the joys which transcend human wishes, these it is easy for God to provide, the exercise of whose generosity is greater when no one expects it; moreover, an angel sent from heaven announced this with a peaceful voice as he came: 'On you the Ruler of Olympus has bestowed the band which this ship carries, so that, though suffering shipwreck, it might be driven into no rocks.' Be trustful, these things will be true, nor will I, who have obtained the promises of God, be disappointed by empty hope, and to us has been granted an island which will be our harbor, in whose anchorage it will be permitted us to enjoy the land we have laid hold of and to look upon the grievous disaster of the broken-up ship without danger."

With these words the wrath of the sea subsided, and at long last the light which had been withdrawn shone aloft; the veil of night having been opened, friendly Malta, which is close to the Sicilian shore by rowing, seemed to disclose to the sailors the land which it provided. But before they should overcome the rabid raging of the sea, Paul cried out, "Break your fast, you weary men, and now taste bread on the fourteenth day," he said, "just as I am eating."

Let us examine by what formula the memorable mysteries of the godly figure have significance: the multitude was ordered to be fed from the flesh of a lamb at that time when the lights of the first month shone forth, on the day proceeding from this number [fourteen]; when the protection of this [flesh] had been tasted,[81] the free [multitude] deserved to avoid the darkness of the Nile;[82] hence Paul at a like interval persuades those whom he wishes to take out of the sea of the world to feast with him and to taste sacred food, following the esteemed footsteps of Moses; to those looking intently at their [Moses' and Paul's] act, these two things are different in their locations but alike in their causes, and the repeated deliverance is raised out of one font:[83] in it Christ is the Lamb, [and] Christ too is considered the Bread from heaven, which He Himself also teaches;[84] he who will have consumed Jesus in his body is free from the Enemy, nor do Pharaoh and Egypt now keep their powers; immediately all the weapons of the demon are sunk in these waters, from which he who had been a captive is reborn as a child; the surge of the salty depths is also left behind, and the marshes of the foul serpent are overcome, and Christ lavishes pastures upon His rescued flock, in their own names,[85] a true Shepherd to him who now eats. Hence also the golden moon bears an allegory of the Church, which is now seen full on the fourteenth day from the first rising of [this] lamp, because [the Church] waxed from the body of Jesus to make in its disk the everlasting light.

Concerning the occasion on which, while Saint Paul was gathering brushwood for a fire on the island of Malta, a snake seized his hand; though the natives called him a murderer and believed that he would die, he threw the snake into the fire; they so marvelled that he was unharmed that they called him a god, [since] they had thought he would die as soon as the swelling came upon him. [1156-1205; Acts 28]

To drive away the cold arising from rain-clouds, Paul had gathered brushwood for the fires; a snake, bearing the weapons of a demon [and] meeting the rising flames, fastened itself on his hand with ancient savagery and in the fire inflicted a wound by cold poison. You wickedly hurtful serpent, why do you still wish to call [us] back from the Lord and contrive your old pillaging on the newness of the law? O lover of death, whose very parent you are, why do you renew your warfare upon the redeemed? You come as a plunderer, but you lie there as plunder, and, bringing death [from a tree],[86] you are destroyed by the branches of a second tree, o evil one, and since the cross of Christ, death is your portion of the wood.

Not far away from here were men bearing rustic hearts, born of the native race, who together made noise with their fearful murmuring: "It is evident that this man is guilty of the crime of bloodshed [and] is not safe now on any shore; sea and land rage against him." They were discussing human affairs and proving divine things. For the animal hanging from his finger was shaken off [and] cast forth into its pyre; rightly was it returned to the flame which it itself gave earlier; it brought forth the fire of sin from which hell is kept hot; the ice of its poison was warmed [and] dissolved into ashes, and the pride of the cold pestilence perished from heat; here the fire and its whirling steam took unaccustomed strength and carried with them their dry fuel. But you, o faith [of Paul], now melted the Snake away, using your zeal; to you the cold Enemy was subjected, and, making a fire in turn, it burned, with its poisonous coldness smoking.

[The natives] said that when swelling came he would fall down [and die]. How far through the void runs a mind ignorant of the good! At that time the venom was already absent from Paul's body, in that the scaly horror, which the ancient serpent gave [to Adam], departed from his eyes;[87] cleansed in the heavenly river and giving up his limbs to the cross of Christ, he did not know how to die from a snake; this flame [of faith] which devoured the poison took its power from the holy waters; burned by them, [the devil] gasps; he grieves that the old colonists are returning to their fatherland. The youths, marvelling for a long time that [Paul] was standing thus, unharmed, said that he was a god; learn at last, ignorant inhabitant [of Malta], with what power He who brings such things to pass reigns in the heavens, that you should think His servants to be this.

The source of allegory in the gift of a glorious deed must now be discerned more fully: the snake, the origin of death—for death, brought forth on this account, has its name from the bite of the sinner [Adam][88]—being hostile to the righteous wished to restrain the hand, since a "hand" providing fit things is rightly called a [good] "work";[89] let whoever has felt such an enemy shake it off vigorously and burn it in the warmth of the Lord. When he learned that the deceit of approaching peril determined to creep to him, eagerly laying hold of heavenly weapons Paul pressed the deception down in the fire, from the tinder of which the growing faith was kindled, ardor was added to the understanding [of the Maltese], and this heat went forth to the multitudes from the abundance of the font.

Concerning the occasion on which Saint Paul, wintering for three months on the island of Malta, after he healed Publius' father, the first citizen of the same region,[90] *who was despaired of, and other sick people, came to Rome {by} sailing with the blowing of the south wind and passing by various places of the sea and the land. {1206-50; Acts 28}*

For the three winter months in the region of Malta Paul gave help of many kinds, and he relieved Publius' parent from imminent disaster; when this favor was seen, people running headlong from everywhere carried off unexpected healing. In the meantime, there sprouted the leafy foliage of bright spring, in which the earth becomes young again as the old age of frost takes flight, and the south wind, catching up the ship as her sails yielded, provided winged waves in the placid sea. It is fitting that that [wind] should blow which the prophet proclaims with his voice: he sings of the burning vision of faith in the south wind.[91] Even so, passing through each of the many towns in separate districts with gales moderated for our joy, [Paul] came to the lofty pinnacles of exalted Rome.[92]

The account begs [me] more profoundly to say that the two lights of the world [Peter and Paul] came together and from regions so wide chose a single place, through which they, who make all lands bright with the virtues of faith, might unite their stars. Although this circumstance might be elaborated with countless figures, I shall willingly utter only a few things with their [the Apostles'] prompting: Peter rose to be the leader in the body of the Church; turret-crowned, she [Rome] surrounded her head with the regions of the world; the greater things gathered to her, so that all the [episcopal] sees might observe the secure heights of the mistress of the world. More justly present in this [place than in any other city], the preferred [city] which instructs the nations, Paul, chosen to be teacher for the gentiles forever, unleashes the power of his eloquence; and whatever he thunders there, the honor of the City compels the subject world to hear. And to overcome Caesar's threats and unfold the laws of heaven in the tyrant's [Nero's] citadel and conquer the highest tribunal in their contest, so that an unimportant enemy should not seize their glory, is a matter worthy of the crown of Peter and Paul.

Egypt bears an image of the world: the people who deserved to be called from there were committed to two leaders for whom a fraternal origin bound their duties together.[93] The great number of idols at Rome, which had been gathered from a conquered world, were crushing hearts addicted to darkness; and this free people, whom Pharaoh [the devil] had previously fettered, put off the shadows of Egypt under the same number of leaders, and through the baptism of God, which at that time the prefiguring sea provided,[94] [this people], obtaining the path of life, found heavenly food. In these [Apostles] also there was a brotherly love; their conduct imparted [this] in them more fully than nature; not the same but a single day presented them to heaven as twins, and [Paul's] passion has made sacred a day repeated in the revolving time of a year, and their conjoined grace gains the everlasting palm.[95]

Notes for Book II

[1]8: The city was sacred to Venus.

[2]33-37: That is, the experience of blindness taught Paul to appreciate better what the senses cannot know; and hence the rightness of his blinding the magician.

[3]59: Ex. 16:14-15.

[4]78-81: Acts 13:25.

[5]84-87: 1 Cor. 10:2-4.

[6]88: Habbac. 1:5, Num. 14:11, Isa. 43:10.

[7]92: Remission of sins, a pure way of life, and then life eternal (gloss); cf. 1.927-30, 1038-41.

[8]115-16: Ps. 15:10.

[9]126-27: Deut. 4:24-26.

[10]135-37: Isa. 42:6, 49:6; Luke 2:32; Acts 13:46-50.

[11]141 ff.: Gen. 25:22-23.

[12]151-52: Jacob, as Esau prefigures Judea.

[13]206-07: See 1.244 ff.

[14]220-23: Matt. 9:27-31.

[15]225: Or, worlds (*orbes*).

[16]231: The "figure" (*imago*) is that of the Church, the Body of

Christ.

[17]236-37: Isa. 52:7; cf. 1.378-79.

[18]242: Acts 14:19.

[19]249-50: John 11:25.

[20]255: Cf. Job 30:7.

[21]283-86: Gen. 17:9-14.

[22]290-91: Gen. 24:1-16.

[23]294-95: Either Christ or Abraham (Heb. 2:16).

[24]322-23: Luke 9:56.

[25]328-31: Luke 9:57-58 (cf. Matt. 8:19-20), Luke 5:27-28.

[26]334-36: Matt. 7:6.

[27]342: Ex. 28.

[28]355: Other than Aaron's (Num. 16:40).

[29]358-59: 1 Tim. 3:2, Tit. 1:7-8.

[30]370: Gal. 4:19.

[31]382: Such as the Asians, returning us to the "frequent question" about God's mercy.

[32]397: That Paul is the servant of God.

[33]409: The spiritual blindness of the crowd.

[34]411: The other meaning of *carcer* (prison).

[35]439: Supposedly the meaning of "Adam."

[36]448: *Fruitur*, an example of the frequent agricultural imagery, here at the prompting of Acts.

[37]455: Mythical first king of Athens.

[38]462-63: Cf. 1 Tim. 4:5.

[39]485-86: Gen. 49:27.

[40]499-500: Gal. 5:17.

[41]501: 1 Cor. 15:10.

[42]502-03: John 14:6.

[43]528: The name means "eagle," and the following pertains to that bird.

[44]541: *Lumine solis* echoes Virgil (*Aen.* 7.130), but the idea is derived from Mal. 4:2, where the *sol iustitiae* was identified with Christ.

[45]548-49: Ps. 102:5.

[46]528-50: The source of this bestiary lore, and its moralization, is the *Physiologus*; cf. Pseudo-Jerome, *Epist.* 18 (*PL* 30, 194).

[47]577-78: Cf. Acts 19:9, 13.

[48]584-88: Matt. 3.

[49]593-95: Matt. 28:19.

[50]597: Mark 1:8.

[51]598: Again, Mark 1:8.

[52]604 ff.: This murky passage upholds the orthodox view that

the unworthiness of the minister does not affect the validity of the sacraments. The Donatists rebaptized those converted to their schismatic sect, maintaining just the opposite opinion. Cf. 1.958-65.

[53]620-22: The Apostles are compared to the twelve baskets full of fragments after the miracle of the loaves and fishes (Matt. 14:20-22).

[54]677-81: Lev. 25:10 ff.

[55]683-87: As the ark, "low in [some glosses insist 'raised above'] the waters," was a kind of island, so that which it prefigured, the Church, is likewise land washed by the saving waters. Cf. 1.643 ff.

[56]700: Household gods.

[57]731-32: Job 28:12-17, Wisd. 7:9, Ps. 11:7.

[58]735: Ex. 25:3.

[59]746: Cf. Rom. 10:10.

[60]774-75: John 10:7.

[61]822-23: Eph. 5:14.

[62]837-42: Matt. 25:14-30, Luke 16:1-12.

[63]865-66: 1 Cor. 3:7.

[64]870-71: Cf. Acts 20:34; as a gloss observes, this is metalepsis, wherein the central term in an extended metaphor is omitted. The meaning is that his own hands have furnished whatever he and his companions needed.

[65]879: Matt. 25:40.

[66]890-91: Cf. The Epistle to Vigilius, 21-22.

[67]892-93: John 2:6.

[68]894-95: 1 Kings 10:3.

[69]895-97: Luke 11:5.

[70]902-04: Matt. 5:41.

[71]909: Matt. 3:10.

[72]910: Luke 13:7.

[73]919-22: 2 Tim. 2:9.

[74]966-67: Gen. 3:7.

[75]973: In the case of Stephen and now with Paul.

[76]976-80: Arator is dealing with the apparent contradiction between Acts 22:9 and 9:7.

[77]1008-10: Ex. 34:28.

[78]1010-13: Ex. 16:14, 35; Num. 20:11.

[79]1048: That is, Felix lost his felicity.

[80]1066: That is, Roman (gloss).

[81]1135: Or, sprinkled (*tacto*); they were both to eat the lamb and to sprinkle its blood on the doorposts.

[82]1133-36: Ex. 12:1-13.

[83]1142: Because both involved passage over a sea.

[84]1144: John 6:35.

[85]1151: John 10:3.

[86]1164: Gen. 3:1.

[87]1184-86: A reference to the conversion that began with his blindness.

[88]1196-97: *Mors* (death)/*morsus* (bite): Adam bit the forbidden fruit.

[89]1198-99: "Work" is a sense shared by *manus* (otherwise "hand") and *opus*.

[90]*Capit*. 1206/2: According to Luke, Publius and not his father was "chief man of the island" (Acts 28:7).

[91]1214-15: Cf. Ezech. 17:10, Ps. 125:4.

[92]1218: With this, Arator takes leave of Acts.

[93]1238-39: The brothers Moses and Aaron (Ex. 4, 5).

[94]1244: 1 Cor. 10:1-4.

[95]1247-50: A tradition held that Peter and Paul were martyred in Rome on the same day, but a year apart. They had a common feast day (June 29).

The Epistle to Parthenius

The Epistle to Parthenius

To the illustrious lord, most magnificent and exalted Parthenius, Master of the Offices[1] *and Patrician, the subdeacon Arator {gives greeting}.*

If, o great one, I should wish to recount the public offices of your progenitors, a page, [though] read on the back, would scarcely furnish [sufficient] space. Great on account of your forefathers and ancestors, you surpass your pedigree by your character, and your origin gives way to your merits, most excellent Parthenius, for whom the name, set down from eternity, is more truly praise for a soul, o chaste one, in which you are pleasing.[2] The tongue as a herald attested the chastity which was to come, and as glory for both [name and person], what you are named you are.

You wear many sword-belts,[3] but *you* make them weighty, for each honor that is given to you soon grows in itself. Who may sing so many good things? I speak briefly; you alone have in you all the things which separately make men great. You, eloquent one, resound among the troops of the Rhône and the Rhine; the royal court approves you as a sweet-voiced man.[4] Germania, splendid indeed in many things, looks up to you as learned, and it rejoices in you with parental love; for her, the greatest glory shines forth from such a son; the thick toga offers [glory] of this kind in the forum of Romulus. I myself saw you, I saw you, young man that you were, on equal terms through your accomplished speech with aged nobles of Italy; having discharged the office of ambassador there, you were sent as an advocate to request the power of independence. You soothed the ears of the Getae with propitious words,[5] and the promises of the people helped your land. That king, in whose control that case then was, could refuse nothing as he heard you [and] applauded.

As soon as Fame, flying forth, began to spread these things abroad in her swift progress and lifted her head with eager ear, the richness of [your] solid eloquence went out among the peoples, and the anxious throng crowded your steps, so that, as often as you opened up rivers by the movement of your lips, [the throng] ran as if to slake a summer thirst. I, eager to touch these riches of language with which, o man of great value, you flow like a wave of the Tagus, was present as a guest gaping at you night and day, since we were kept in these dwellings[6] in the city of Ravenna. What books, what names you sounded forth to me, o learned one! At the same time, recalling so much, you were the image of a book! There for the first time I read under your guidance the *Histories* of Caesar, which he composed for himself as journals.[7] You used to recite with a calm and pleasing charm the poets in whom was a deceitful art, a proud display. But nevertheless, o most excellent one, you kept returning to the true bards whose lute[8] draws the meters to its own laws, such as Ambrose, who excels in the Hyblaean hymns which you, o bees, foreshowed to him lying in the cradle;[9] such as Decentius,[10] who abounded in this same art, and you, o Sidonian lyre, [who] sing among the people of Auvergne.[11]

It had long been my concern in the youthful years to pursue continual song in my verses, to write of the roles which myth invented, and to be carried off in the power of shallowness through an empty channel. When my fragile reed had sung these things to you, and dear friend, your love was often supporting me, you said, "Oh, would that you had chosen more properly to turn the path of this voice toward praises of the Lord! so that, as you have the name by which we call you, Arator,[12] the crop might not have been hidden, but instead accessible to you." I resolved, I admit, that if ever I deserved by some chance to follow the rewards[13] of my talent to better things, the work which I sang should be sent to wherever it should happen for you to be, o best of men. Now the promised day spurs me to wish finally to dissolve my debts and my contracts, o learned one. Take the song which I have skimmed from a glistening sea, and graciously accept the waters, meager though they be. There remains in that expanse a deep ocean of matters from which I have barely drawn a scant drop with my mouth.[14]

For I, united with the pleasant sheep-folds of the Roman Church, made a sheep by my tonsured head, seeing the rich pastures and sunny volumes of Christ, sought to eat all things in my sampling and at one moment, accustomed to the flowers of David, to consume songs; at another my gluttonous mind desired Genesis. And since I prefer to graze at one and the same time on violets and lilies which an old and a new scent combined, there occured to me that [book] which the Canon names Acts, a book filled with the Apostles' harvest in the world, in which the heavenly Lord, with

Peter as His fisherman, raised us up from the bosom of the salty, sky-blue sea and, an allegory having been disclosed, gave [Peter] a ship [the Church] to satisfy their hunger for the nations who were taken up in it.[15]

I, a novice, produced poetry from this man's story and carefully gave the words to my shepherd, who very amply brings new words to the singer with his help; without this [help] from him, no one can speak worthy things; these [poems] were openly handed over to our illustrious Father the Pope, and the hidden archives[16] of the Church duly contain [them].

Come then! Let your conversation honor the books which have been received. The heavenly cause will pay the wages of my salary, because there are bishops in the Master's religion, many good men whom learned Gaul offers; Firminus is there, that venerable priest, who will feed the people with words of doctrine. His praise extends to the territory of Italy, and his glory is honored beyond his native land.

Doubt not that the lessons which have been pleasing to the man of the Apostolic See will be acceptable to the worthy; nor certainly should you think that you will be without the reward of fame, because you are displaying there these writings prefixed to my work. Together we shall both pass to the place where that poem will have arrived, and [where] the Parthenian glory will always be on men's lips.[17]

Notes for the Epistle to Parthenius

[1]The *Magister Officiorum* oversaw most other servants of the emperor or king. Parthenius was probably in Burgundy at the time. Arator had known him during his days in Ravenna, where Parthenius, who seems to have distinguished himself in rhetoric, guided the young man during his experiments with poetry. Arator promised that if he ever wrote a worthy poem on a Christian theme he would send it to Parthenius, wherever he might be. At first undecided over which Testament should supply the matter, Arator settled upon Acts. The work was finished at the beginning of 544. It was offered to the Pope, and parts of it were read to an assembly of the clergy. Vigilius then had it placed in the papal archives. But learned Romans clamored for a public recitation; their request was approved, and Arator himself read it. This epistle is found in only two MSS and has no commentary; moreover, McKinlay has provided no

notes for it under "De Locis Criticis." There is independent evidence of Parthenius' stay in Gaul, and his demise is recorded in that chamber of horrors by Gregory of Tours, *The History of the Franks* (3.36).

[2]6: The Greek for "virginity" is *partheneia*.

[3]9: *Cingula*, symbols of office.

[4]13-14: Probably during his stay in Burgundy.

[5]23: An embassy to an unknown Gothic (?) king.

[6]35: Or (less likely), by these household deities (*Lares*).

[7]39-40: The reference is to Caesar's *Commentaries*.

[8]44: So McKinlay (p. 286), but more likely "faith" (*fides*).

[9]45-46: Bees were said to have settled in Ambrose's mouth while he was sleeping in the cradle, foreshadowing the sweetness of his hymns. Hybla was a Sicilian mountain range famous in antiquity for its bees.

[10]47: Decentius is unidentified; it is most likely that Arator intended Dracontius, whose epic *De Laudibus Dei* was composed ca. 490.

[11]48: Sidonius (ca. 430-ca. 479), poet and bishop of the Arverni.

[12]57: That is, Farmer.

[13]60: *Fructus*.

[14]65-68: Cf. The Epistle to Florianus, 7-8.

[15]81-82: Cf. *De Actibus* 1.887-913.

[16]88: Taking *scrinia condita* as nominative.

[17]102: Taking *Parthenium decus* as nominative.